The Authors

Wayne C. Mannebach is Associate Professor of Speech and Director of Forensics at Ripon College, Ripon, Wisconsin. A graduate of Wisconsin State University at Oshkosh, he earned his M.A. and his Ph.D. from Ohio University in the field of Rhetoric and Public Address. In addition to his classroom responsibilities, he has conducted many special courses in public speaking for professional groups including clergymen. He has also been an instructor in Speech and TV Communication for the Upward Bound Program held at Ripon College during four summer sessions.

Joseph M. Mazza is Professor of Speech and the Coordinator of Rhetoric and Public Address in the Speech Department of Wisconsin State University at Oshkosh. He earned the bachelor's and master's degree from Marquette University and the doctorate at the University of Wisconsin. He has conducted homiletical workshops for clergymen of all faiths. He formerly taught speech at Marquette University and Yankton College in South Dakota.

Speaking from the Pulpit

From two laymen commited to improving communications between clergymen of all faiths and their listeners.

Speaking from the Pulpit

Wayne C. Mannebach
Joseph M. Mazza

Judson Press, Valley Forge

SPEAKING FROM THE PULPIT

The Judson Press
Valley Forge, Pa. 19481

Standard Book No. 8170-0437-8
Library of Congress Catalog Card No. 74-81445

Printed in the U.S.A.

Preface

THE CONCEPTION OF THIS BOOK grew out of our study and observations of the public speaking of preachers from various denominations and out of our opportunities to work with pastors in programs designed to improve their preaching abilities. This book is designed especially for those clergymen who clearly are mistaken in believing that because they speak from a pulpit and treat Holy Scripture, their audiences automatically listen with acute attention and are influenced by their verbal and visual presentations. Clergymen assume the mandate to preach in a world of reality, and it is our desire to contribute to the improvement of pulpit discourse within this context.

The clergy should always remember that effective communication demands subject matter which is appropriate to the speaker, to the audience, and to the occasion for speaking; that effective communication demands that religious concepts be supported with creditable evidence, valid logical processes, well-grounded emotional appeals, and speaking behavior which displays the speaker's intelligence, character, and goodwill; that effective communication demands precision in structure; that effective communication demands a style which generates clarity and impressiveness of thought; and that effective communication demands vocal and visual presentations which enhance the speaker's thoughts.

The focus of this book is selective, in the hope that it soon reaches those preachers who are involved regularly in the speaker-audience situation. We are aware that clergymen do not always face a speaker-audience situation but that they frequently communicate in intimate small-group and mass-media situations. We also are aware that clergymen sometimes are more influential in one situation than in another, and sometimes are influential in their actions without the necessity of the spoken word.

This book treats the constituents of effective communication in such a manner that clergymen of all faiths may find time to read and comprehend it. The authors hope that those clergymen who for a long time have not met the needs of their audiences will care to improve, soon generating in those congregations a desire to listen, adhere, and put into practice the precepts emanating from the pulpit.

WAYNE C. MANNEBACH
JOSEPH M. MAZZA

August 1, 1969

Contents

1
The Condition of the Audience

THIRTY CLERGYMEN OF DIFFERENT DENOMINATIONS recently were asked to identify significant problems they encountered while speaking to their congregations. They revealed that the people who attend their services not only represent innumerable facets of society but also are inconsistent in their attendance, so that the clergymen rarely can predict with accuracy the composition of an audience for a given service.

THE PROBLEM OF AUDIENCE HETEROGENEITY

The problem most alluded to was the heterogeneity of the audiences. Perhaps the only deduction a preacher can make about any given congregation is that the people have some interest in religion, but even this factor prompts a response that says there are differences of interest in religion for everyone. This is a problem that has been as widespread historically as it is today. For example, Joseph Glanvill, a seventeenth-century Anglican preacher, once remarked that some people came to church to be entertained while others came with a distorted zeal for religion. In his *Seasonable Defence of Preaching,* Glanvill set up a typology of religious audiences, using anonymous characters in dialogue fashion to represent the different types in an audience. Each type identified by Glanvill has a counterpart in today's church congregations.

Glanvill presented five characters labeled A, B, C, D, and E. Character A represented the Anglican layman who ideally defended the conformist ministry. However, Character A was not always a model churchgoer, nor was he successful in persuading other laymen to concur in his religious convictions about the Anglican Church. Character B represented those people who believed there was too much preaching in the world. Character B was not totally opposed to preaching, but he contended that reliance upon frequent preaching as a tool by which men were won to the faith led to contempt and disbelief. Character C represented those people who preferred the homilies, prayers, and catechetical instruction prescribed in the *Book of Common Prayer* rather than sermons composed by the minister. Character C contended that preaching had little value, for the preacher was unable to change the nature of the hearers. Character D represented the laymen who broke away from the established church, turned to nonconformist sects for spiritual gratification, and indicted the clergy for preaching erroneous doctrine. Character E represented the Anglican laymen who belonged to a parish in which the minister's reading of the prescribed homilies of the Anglican Church was a substitute for plain preaching. Character E criticized other members of the laity on the grounds that they were insincere in their devotion and lacked the intelligence to understand divine matters.[1]

Other clergymen have written about this problem, but little has been said about how to confront it today. Evidence reveals that too many resign themselves to the condition of excessive diversity within their audiences and confess their inability to cope with it. They can begin to confront this problem by gaining specific knowledge of their entire congregations.

NOW YOU SEE THEM

Most clergymen have access to information about their congregations, but few utilize this information so as to know at least the statistics about their congregations and to identify patterns that are based on the information. For example, some of the data that can be gathered and collated are:

1. *Age*. How many members of the congregation fall into the following brackets: 1-7, 8-14, 15-18, 19-21, 22-25, 26-30, 31-40, 41-50, 51-60, 61-65, 66 and over? Where are the concentrated populations?
2. *Sex*. How many men and women are in each age bracket? What patterns appear in the statistics? For example, are there more men than women under the age of thirty?

3. *Marital status.* How many single men and women are there in the group? How many fall in each age bracket? How many married couples are there, and what age brackets do they represent? How many divorced people and remarried people are there? How many children? How many widows and widowers? How many adopted or foster children?
4. *Employment.* How do the people earn a living? How many blue-collar and white-collar positions do they hold? Is there a certain type of employment that predominates? How many teachers, doctors, dentists, lawyers, and factory workers belong? How many women are working, and are these single or married? If married, do they have children?
5. *Economic status.* What are the various incomes of the people, and how many are in each category? How many people own their homes?
6. *Ethnic and race.* What races are represented in the congregation? What ethnic groups are represented, and how many are in each group? Are there interracial marriages? How many?
7. *Organizational affiliations.* What religious organizations or clubs do the people represent? What sex or age groups predominate in such organizations? How many people belong to civic organizations? How many espouse the various political parties or ideologies? Is there a predominant political ideology?
8. *Educational background.* How many have been graduated from grade school, high school, college, and professional and graduate schools? How many had public, parochial, or private-school formal education, and for how many years?

Once the pastor has collected and arranged this data into patterns, he should refer to it when preparing his sermons, for sermons should be designed for a specific congregation, not a universal one. By relying on his congregational profile, the preacher is less likely to address an age bracket that is not in his audience, or to talk as though the majority of his hearers were wealthy when the contrary is true. Moreover, he is more likely to be cognizant of any exception to the general patterns, especially of the religious implications involved.

It is insufficient for the man in the pulpit to look at his hearers once a week and rationalize that they are all the same in the eyes of God — and then proceed to communicate as though the people were all of one age, sex, marital status, economic status, educational level, and political or religious ideology. While most clergymen are mildly aware that similarities and differences exist in their congregations, few have a precise knowledge of these factors and fewer adapt to these realities in the preparation of their sermons and other discourses about religion. They certainly assume the responsibility to preach as mediators between God and man, but the influence of communication among human beings is not fully realized when God's words are preached downwardly from the clergy to the laity. In this sense the clergyman follows a pattern of one-way communication: from God, to the pulpiteer, and then to the laity. When preparing to preach, the clergyman should conceive of himself as being the mediator between God and his *real* congregation for a meaningful three-way communication. The preacher serves this role best when he accounts for his congregation as he *finds* and *knows* them, not as he *thinks* they are or should be.

When the preacher has knowledge regarding any one category, he is more likely to observe the potential for many sermons about age and religion, education and religion, or all other categories and their religious implications. Also, given any concept in religious discourse, the clergyman will see that it may have a relationship to all or most categories. For example, the general topic of crime and what religion has to say about it generates a variety of specific concepts about crime. Further, some perspectives are crime and age brackets, crime and sex, crime and education, crime and employment, crime and race, and crime and group affiliations. The preacher can better focus on these perspectives if he has a profile of data about his congregation.

In practice, clergymen generally note and adapt to some of the most obvious similarities that exist, but all too often they fail to observe and to account for the *differences* that exist. For example, when a clergyman recently addressed a group of fathers and sons, he spent most of his time discussing the problems of parents in rearing their children. He apparently failed to account for the younger half of his audience, as is shown by the reaction of one teen-age son who said after the experience: "After the speech there was a question and answer session that proved to be a slight success. The audience participated in the discussion, but the opinions were one-sided. The fathers were the only ones who spoke, and the sons were afraid to voice their reactions. The speech would have had greater success if the fathers and sons were separated."

Some clergymen attempt to control the diversity of congregations by employing practices that may or may not be useful. For example, some schedule services for different age groups. Some advertise on religious billboards and in bulletins and newspapers their sermon topics and the intended audiences. Some look for patterns of attendance by certain people at certain times, and adapt their sermons to the anticipated group. Others attempt to adapt their message to diverse congregations through internal identification of the groups. Thus, it is common to hear a preacher direct certain portions of his sermon to the young, the old, and the married people present. There is little evidence to believe that one approach is necessarily better than another. The clergyman who aims at influencing the religious beliefs and actions of his congregation should try several approaches. But before he attempts to preach, he should begin with a profile of congregational data as a reference point.

Some pastors have commented that they conduct religious instructional services for each of the various age groups, and therefore these people are receiving intensive religious instruction. Such reasoning has prompted some preachers to ignore these people in their sermons. Other clergymen have commented that the family is the basic unit, and therefore they have directed their sermons to the family unit. Both of these attitudes result in preaching practices that ignore conscious and rational audience analysis. The presumption that religious instructions are the same as preaching loses sight of the fact that instruction often is limited to exposure to, or drill in, the tenets and historical data of a specific denomination. There is also the presumption that, if religious instruction is offered early in life, the recipient will apply it for the rest of his life. But many a clergyman fails to give religious instruction outside of the regular services, and because of this the only contact with him for many people is the regular service in which the sermon occurs. With respect to the family unit comment, to direct a sermon constantly to the family unit is to overlook potentially significant factors that may exist and be important at the time of the sermon. This, too, reflects a lack of knowledge about the significant differences and similarities that may exist in the composition of the entire congregation, or of one specific group within the congregation.

NOW YOU DON'T

A knowledge of the external characteristics of a given congregation is relatively easy to gather and examine, but there are factors operating in the speaking situation that are not clearly observable. The counterpart of speaking is listening, and preachers may better prepare their sermons if they are aware of the probable thoughts of the audience during a given sermon.

Ralph Nichols has reflected extensively on the subject of listening. He makes the speaker acutely aware of some of the behavior of listeners and generally advocates education for the masses on how to listen in society.[2] Perhaps it is impractical for busy pastors to instruct their congregations on how to listen, but there may be some innovative ones who care to do something about it when and where they are able.

Some people who attend church services are uninterested in the substance of the sermon. After they learn what the sermon is about, they suddenly lose all interest in the rest of it. This is a factor that preachers must consider when preparing their sermons. Other people may lack motivation to listen, and this should prompt preachers to consider the motivational bases for their sermons. Concepts that generally are appealing to people are discussed in Chapter 2, whereas certain motivational bases for speaking and listening will be treated in Chapters 3 and 4. The immediate point is that listening is a silent process, and lack of interest in the clergy's concepts leads to low levels of attention.

Other listeners tend to correlate ineffective oral and visual habits of delivery with the substance of the sermon. If they do not like the preacher's vocal or physical behavior, they often rationalize that they dislike the substance of the sermon. Thus, it is essential that the clergyman consider what he can do to improve his delivery. A thought-provoking preacher, observing that there are some preachers who say very little but are visually or vocally dynamic, may conclude that his delivery is of no consequence. Ministers often tend to believe that religious ideas will prevail in spite of ineffective delivery. Nonetheless, investigation reveals that the human behavior of the listener often is influenced more by delivery than by any other component of oral communication. (Effective delivery is more fully treated in Chapter 6.)

Clergymen address audiences which contain people who are easy and people who are difficult to excite intellectually and emotionally. If a member of a congregation is easy to excite, he may concentrate on something which the preacher has described, and his resulting excitement over it causes him to fail to listen attentively to subsequent communication. Such a person can put himself through a process of mental introspection and shut out the world immediately adjacent to him. Likewise, there are people who are so predisposed to preaching that they have a low level of expectation of help or inspiration from sermons. Such people have developed a patterned behavior in which they have acclimated themselves to being comfortable in the listening situation. They are so familiar with the preaching of a particular clergyman that they seem to build up an immunity against his preaching over a period of time.

Professor Nichols revealed that good listeners tend to focus on central ideas, but only about 25 percent of persons listening to a formal talk are able to grasp the speaker's central idea. Professor Nichols recommends the employment of conventional organizational thought-patterns, transitional language, and recapitulation to increase the listener's ability to locate the important ideas in a given discourse.[3] It is important for the clergyman to use tools of discourse to create conceptual focus for the members of his congregation. (Structure is discussed in Chapter 4.)

Human behavior is such that attention can be faked in the listening situation. Many people tend to exert themselves to concentrate on the sermon, if for no other reason than out of respect for the preacher. Then, at any given point in the oral-aural situation the listener's mind can go in one direction while his physical symptoms would lead one to believe that he is attending to what is being said. The religious arena is not exempt from this listening habit. There are other people who choose not to feign attention. For example, one person commented after a Christmas sermon:

> His language was clear in conveying his meaning, but it sounded as if his only motivation was that he had to give a sermon. The members of the congregation were looking around, staring at the floor, and in general not paying attention. Consequently the application of his Christmas message was lost to many in attendance.

The zealous preacher may over-react to this phenomenon of latent attention by employing all kinds of devices for grasping and sustaining the attention of his audience. Perhaps nothing could be more disastrous, for he may succeed in keeping his listeners awake but fail to influence their religious thought and behavior. The danger is that the preacher may concentrate his energy on one aspect of speaking while he excludes a comprehensive approach to homiletic preparation. Serious preparation of the inventive, stylistic, structural, and oral-visual aspects of the sermon tends to increase the amount of real attention by the listener.

Distraction is another phenomenon that occurs in the listening situation. People are notorious for mentally creating their own distractions. For example, when a sermon becomes dull, the listener can think about some problem or some pleasant experience he or she is having. People who need relief from sleep-inducing sermons also find distractions in the physical surroundings, such as the clothing of certain people, the beautiful church windows, or the numerous items of the church's aids to worship. Many churches have eliminated the distractions of crying babies and noisy children by building soundproof rooms or by providing baby-sitting service. This device may eliminate certain obvious distractions, but the silent potential for distraction is much more difficult to combat. There is constant need for preachers to make certain that their sermons relate directly to the reality of the audience. In this way they minimize the boundaries of silent fantasy and other processes of distraction.

The last phenomenon concerns the ability of the listening mind to receive discourse at a rate relatively faster than is commonly expected. Many clergymen think that in order to be understood they must speak very slowly. Chapter 6 on the subject of delivery discusses this point, but it is important to know that technically the mind is faster than the tongue. Sometimes a faster rate of speaking may help to sustain attention, and it certainly allows the clergyman to cover more substance in a given amount of time. It is conceivable that the clergy could lessen the time normally given to a sermon and be just as effective. The era is over when the hourglass determines the length of the sermon.

2
The Conceptual Process

There are many occasions when clergymen have little or no control over the subjects of their speeches. This is true when they are invited to speak to certain groups on subjects dictated by the program chairmen. For example, one clergyman was invited by a Rotary Club chapter to describe his experiences in living for nearly ten years among primitive tribes in Africa. Another was invited to explain to a Parent-Teacher Association meeting the moral implications of certain motion pictures and television shows. Some are compelled by their church hierarchies to adhere to a lectionary or syllabus established for the church year. And some clergymen must speak on subjects determined by their immediate superiors, among whom are pastors and even committees composed of laymen. In such situations the preachers have to determine only what aspects of the subjects they will cover, thus tailoring their topics to conform to the requirements established by their superiors or by the groups that invited them to speak.

THE CLERGYMAN'S STOREHOUSE

Many ministers are entirely free to select their own subjects for speaking. Because of the numerous opportunities for speaking and the lack of guidelines in the selection of subject matter, two questions commonly occur to the preacher. The first question is: "What should I talk about?" The second question is: "Where can I get material for my speech?" To answer these questions preachers should immediately turn to their own storehouses of potential subject matter. Each storehouse may be divided into at least three compartments of potential subject matter: personal experiences, social experiences, and scriptural experiences.

1. *Personal experiences.* The world in which most clergymen live is abundant with subjects on which they can speak with personal authority. For example, the clergyman can base his sermons and other public addresses on his personal experiences with dope addicts, chronic alcoholics, rapists, the mentally retarded, the criminally insane, prostitutes, the unemployed, the impoverished, unwed mothers, atheists, and people who know they are dying of incurable diseases. He can talk about his trips to Alaska, Hawaii, London, Rome, Paris, the Netherlands, India, Japan, Hong Kong, Vietnam, and Thailand. Within the above addresses the preacher can touch upon man's duties to God, to himself, to his family, and to society in general. Such examples demonstrate that personal experiences are potential subject matter for speeches.

2. *Social experiences.* The world today offers unlimited subjects on which the clergy may speak. Potential social subject matters are racial disharmony, the threat of communism, the generation gap, the war on poverty, world population, foreign aid, the ethics of advertising, the space race, the rising costs of living, the future of religion, and the war on organized crime. To be sure, many clergymen can speak on these subjects from personal experience, but even those preachers who have not personally experienced certain phenomena operating in society may talk about them with authority by conducting careful research and gathering information from reputable journals, magazines, bulletins, reviews, newsletters, and books. Appendix I represents only a small portion of the numerous sources of subject matter for sermons, discussions, and other forms of oral communication.

3. *Scriptural experiences.* It is assumed that all ministers are familiar with the general content of Scripture and thus have no difficulty in finding particular passages. However, clergymen often find it difficult to discover fresh approaches to the treatment of Scripture. Congregations do not expect to listen to the same sermons year after year; they demand variety of subject matter. To provide this variety when treating Scripture, preachers should turn to one or several of the works that deal with the history and interpretation of Scripture. Appendix II represents

only a few of the many works that are easily available and are helpful to those who are looking for fresh subject matter for their sermons and other forms of oral communication.

One problem a preacher should not have is being unable to find subjects on which to speak. The information contained in the Appendixes is too complete to allow a preacher to say, "Why, I don't know what to talk about." The famous orator Booker T. Washington once remarked:

> A ship lost at sea for many days suddenly sighted a friendly vessel. From the mast of the unfortunate vessel was seen a signal: "Water, water; we die of thirst!" The answer from the friendly vessel at once came back: "Cast down your bucket where you are." A second time the signal, "Water, water; send us water!" ran up from the distressed vessel, and was answered: "Cast down your bucket where you are." . . . The captain of the distressed vessel, at last heeding the injunction, cast down his bucket, and it came up full of fresh, sparkling water from the mouth of the Amazon River.[1]

Those who lack subjects on which to speak may be compared to the occupants aboard the distressed vessel alluded to by Washington. If such clergymen would "cast down their buckets" in their personal, social, and scriptural experiences, they would come up full of "fresh, sparkling" subject matter.

THE IMPORTANCE CONTINUUM

As stated earlier, preparing for a sermon involves the perspectives of audience analysis and the preacher's storehouse of potential subject matter. When the preacher has selected a specific subject, he should consciously examine the subject by asking himself: *Is this subject important or significant to this congregation?* The facile answer is "yes," for preachers are tempted to believe that anything they talk about in the pulpit is important. The difficult answer is to establish the reason why the subject is important to the particular congregation at the particular time. The subject may be important to the clergyman, but unimportant to the congregation. All too often, clergymen assume that because people attend church they therefore consider as important everything pertaining to religion. Such is not the case.

The ultimate determination of subject significance should be the acknowledgment of shared experience. Both the clergyman and his congregation should come to share a religious experience, for effective communication involves the audience as well as the speaker. However, too often the clergyman not only ignores the audience when selecting his subject, but also fails to control subject selection. For example, the subject matter of sermons frequently is determined by the particular denomination; topics are designated, planned annually, and disseminated to the clergy. Arbitrary selection of subject matter without regard for its importance to the particular audience can easily result in sterile communication. Automatic selection of a theme based upon Scripture and prescribed for a given day also negates the consideration of the importance of the audience.

One clergyman recently spoke to four hundred college students on the subject, "People Should Look Forward to the Judgment Day." This has been a common subject since the beginning of Christianity, but the speaker made no attempt to focus on the importance of this subject to his specific audience. The practice of selecting a universal subject increases the probability that the development of the subject will not pertain to the immediate audience. When the preacher knows in advance who will constitute his audience, he should phrase and focus the subject in their direction. A simple transposition for the above subject might be, for example, "College Students Should Look Forward to the Judgment Day."

The preaching situation involves both the clergyman and the audience, but the clergyman usually determines the focal point of the sermon. The focal point sometimes is determined by both when a specific situation arises which has religious importance. A eulogy by a clergyman for a member of his congregation is an example of this kind of situation. In times of intense tragedy or crisis both the clergyman and the laity feel a compulsion to share a verbalization of the religious implication of the event. The assassinations of John F. Kennedy, Martin Luther King, Jr., and Robert F. Kennedy represent events of this nature. There are also the subtle, continuing events which do not occur suddenly but which have religious implications. Well-known examples are the continuing military conflict in Vietnam and the racial strife in our society. If the clergyman believes there are sudden or continuing implications or considerations of moral conviction or behavior involved in events like these, he has an obligation to bring his concerns before his congregation.

The importance of sermon subject matter can be judged in light of its specific relevance for the specific audience. The sermon is a unique opportunity for the clergy to be relevant to a specific group. Young people complain about the irrelevance of religion in society and become disenchanted with formalized religion. An echo to "God is dead" is "the sermon is dead." Undoubtedly the preacher wants to avoid comments like the following one made by a young woman: "There was no emotional response after he finished presenting his sermon on 'Peace,' which was based on the scriptural account of Thomas doubting Christ. As usual—it went in one ear and out the other."

People who fail to visit the house of God are another factor for the preacher to consider when he is determining the emphasis of his sermon. People who feel no compulsion to participate in formal religious services may do so because those in the church—pulpit and pew alike—have failed to communicate the relevance of religion for man. Some preachers also concentrate their sermons on the importance of the financial support of the church. While this concept is relevant to reality, it may not be considered important to religion by members of the congregation. The clergy should study the extent of effort spent in sermons on this concept and the possible effect it has in driving people away from formal services. If preachers fail to determine that their sermons are important and relevant to their congregations, they increase the probability that they will lack influence in the whole realm of religious instruction and moral persuasion.

Pulpit discourse traditionally has concerned itself with the dualistic relationship between the individual and God. In contrast, today's sermons must be concerned with the pluralistic relationship between God, the individual, and the reality of this world and its inhabitants. Some people refer to this distinction as the private gospel versus the social gospel. Sermons that reflect the private gospel focus are on such subjects as "We Need to Experience Christ," "If We Know About Christ We Will Care," "We Should Seek Forgiveness of Our Sins," "We Should Repent Through Constant Worship," "We Must Accept Him as Our Savior," and "I Can Do All Things Through Christ." Examples of the social gospel focus are "The Challenge of Black Power" and "The Shadow of War in Vietnam."

There is a strong suspicion that ministers spend too much

time in the pulpit on the private gospel and not enough on the social gospel, so that the application of religious conviction to society is made to seem less important than the application of religion to one's self and perhaps one's immediate family. Another way to look at this dichotomy is that participation in religion occurs formally only on the day of worship while the rest of the week is devoted to secular affairs, devoid of any religious application. Each preacher should examine the extent to which he emphasizes one gospel perspective to the exclusion of the other gospel perspective as a motivating basis for the importance of sermons. A checklist can be made by categorizing one year's sermon subjects into the two groups to determine the numerical frequency of each type.

CONCEPT FOCUS

The following testimonial by one member of a congregation in response to a recent homily describes the "shotgun" approach of some preachers:

> Unfortunately, one cannot say that his primary purpose could readily be seen. In the course of his fifty-minute homily, he jumped from one topic to another. He started with the purpose of giving us the sixth in a series of talks explaining the new liturgy, mass gestures, and responses. However, somewhere along the line, he slid into reprimanding his parishioners for not visiting the ten shut-ins of the parish. This led to another topic, that of thankfulness for our good health and fortune.

While this problem is discussed further in Chapter 4, it is presented here because of its close relationship to audience analysis and concept significance. The above statement implicates the clergyman's lack of conceptual unity and his failure to establish the significance of one focal point. Another layman lamented: "I've already heard clergymen who ramble on about everything from teen-agers to stars."

Another attempt at sermon focus involves the practice of using comparison as the thematic design. Comparison is by its very nature a diffuse process and may have some undesirable effects. For example, after a sermon delivered on Easter Sunday a listener remarked:

> The priest began immediately with his speech by comparing the resurrection of our Lord with the hatching of an egg. I felt that the comparison used was oversimplified and an insult to my intelligence. This priest continued with one comparison after another with no apparent goal. I

> suppose much can be learned from these segments in his sermon, but it seemed to me he was giving ten different sermons all condensed into one. At the end of his sermon I tried to think of all that he had said, and all I could think about was the hatching of the egg.

The result poses a serious question as to whether or not focus was established and the significance of the occasion communicated. Other examples of comparisons in sermons are "Our Christian Life Is like a Mystery Story," and "Our Christian Life Is like Life Aboard a Submarine." The first example compounds the problem that people face in applying religion to reality. It diffuses concept focus, for mysteries are ethereal and defy focus. The second example is a hypothetical experience for most people, and the intensity of focus on submarine life may lose its significance for most members of a congregation.

Four different groups of students at Wisconsin State University in Oshkosh were asked to respond to each of the concepts listed below. They were asked to establish their motivational interest in each idea according to the motivational scale. Specifically they were asked if they would be interested in listening to a speech on each concept and, if so, to what extent. The resultant data have a relevance for most preachers, for the data provide the seeds for potential discourse. The preacher can focus on religious conviction and action based alone upon the interest factor that exists in his congregation. He can carry this process a step further to determine the attitudes of his hearers concerning these concepts by attempting to find out who holds which attitudes and the intensity of the attitudes. The following data only indicate how many persons were interested in hearing a speech about the concepts listed. Each preacher may draw inferences from the concepts and the resultant data as he wishes, but he may find the data useful whenever he prepares a sermon.

Although this rating reflects the attitudes of a limited group, it does demonstrate the need to relate to specific interests.

MOTIVATIONAL SCALE

1. Highly Motivated
2. Moderately Motivated
3. Undecided Motivation
4. Moderately Unmotivated
5. Strongly Unmotivated

	RATING				
CONCEPT	*1*	*2*	*3*	*4*	*5*
I believe in the idea of one common Christian religion.	10	24	17	10	6
The hippie movement is one example of our generation's discontent with society.	15	35	13	3	3
Abortion should be legalized.	23	27	8	1	12
There is a conflict between the new morality and religion.	9	31	12	13	6
There has been a marked increase in suicides in the United States.	12	25	18	9	7
Pornography is a cause of the changing morality in America.	15	30	16	6	4
Couples who do not know each other well before marriage remain strangers after marriage.	13	26	13	11	5
Homosexuality is becoming acceptable in our present society.	20	21	11	10	6
Students of science are beginning to believe there are natural causes behind all religious phenomena.	18	19	17	10	7
It is right to use napalm in war.	18	20	18	9	12
Discrimination exists in the armed forces.	18	24	13	11	4
A person should not feel obligated to attend church on Sundays.	19	17	17	8	10
Religion should be taught in state schools.	16	12	16	12	14
The Government should share its funds between public and parochial schools.	16	19	10	13	13
Capital punishment should be abolished throughout the world.	20	23	9	13	6
There should be an established world-wide religion.	18	17	12	9	15
The Catholic Church should recognize the ultimate necessity of birth control.	27	21	12	6	2

Sex education should be started in junior high schools.	30	22	11	4	3
Church and state should remain separated.	28	14	9	13	6
Premarital sex tends to weaken marriage.	27	19	13	6	5
The motion picture industry is producing films today that are doing great injury.	12	20	11	8	6
LSD is a dangerous drug.	24	26	10	8	3
Vandalism and crime committed by delinquents is increasing in our cities.	17	26	15	5	2
Some advertisements cheat and give us false hopes.	14	29	14	7	5

CHECKLIST FOR SELECTION CRITERIA

In short, the preacher should make certain that he selects concepts of importance and relevance to his congregation, that his sermons account for the reality of his audience, and that the final selection of a concept is based upon an experience shared by the preacher and his audience. To improve concept focus, preachers would be wise to adhere to the following checklist, or to construct a more detailed one.

1. Is this concept important or significant?
2. Is this concept relevant at this time?
3. Do I have a motivational basis for selecting this concept?
4. Does the audience have a motivational basis for listening?
   a. Are they interested?
   b. Do they want or need it?
   c. Does the concept conflict with other wants?
5. Does this concept relate specifically to the reality of the congregation?
6. Do the following factors generate specific concepts?
   a. The age or sex of the audience.
   b. The social, political, or religious attitudes of the audience.
   c. The local background, situation, or events.
   d. The psychological wants and needs of the audience; i.e., security, love, esteem, self-realization.
   e. The cultural patterns of the audience; i.e., political democracy, private property and enterprise, marriage and divorce, race, religion, war and peace.

3
Logos, Pathos, and Ethos

THIS CHAPTER treats the logical, emotional, and ethical modes of persuasion, respectively called *logos, pathos,* and *ethos.*

Fundamentally, the constituents of *logos* are evidence and formal mental processes. Evidence is the raw material used to establish proof. Evidence includes testimony from witnesses, testimony in written form, historical facts, documents, pictorializations, recordings, and relics that induce in the minds of the hearers a tendency to affirm the truth of the proposition to which the evidence attaches and in support of which it is used. Formal mental processes are the utilizations of evidence in forms that lead to conclusions. Inductive processes move from the specific to the general and occur through examples, analogies, and causal relations. Deductive processes move from the general to the specific and occur through syllogisms and enthymemes.

Pathos includes general motivational situations and specific emotional appeals that are calculated to put the audience in a frame of mind suitable for the reception of the speaker's propositions.

Ethos includes those materials that the speaker uses to establish himself as a person of intelligence, moral character, and goodwill, and the attempts of the speaker to use his *ethos* thus gained as a form of persuasive support.

LOGOS

Evidence is the raw material used to establish proof. A speaker who employs evidence implies to his hearers that he does not wish to offer only his ideas on the particular issue, and that he has material that would have been available whether or not he had ever delivered his speech.

Testimony from witnesses refers only to those statements from persons under direct observation by the audience, thus allowing for the possibility of cross-examination. This type of evidence usually appears in courts of law, but it is not atypical to church services. For example, a pastor of a church delivered a sermon in which he urged his hearers to aid the inhabitants of a particular foreign mission. Upon completing his sermon, the pastor introduced to his audience another clergyman who had served at the mission, and who was available to verify anything the pastor had said and to contribute additional information.

Testimony in written form refers to statements from persons not under direct observation by the audience, thus disallowing for the possibility of immediate cross-examination. Most clergymen prefer this type of evidence because of the evidence's availability, mobility, and inexpensiveness.

An example of evidence of historical facts appears in President Roosevelt's address to the American people on the evening of December 8, 1941. The President contended that the course Japan had followed in Asia for the past ten years paralleled the course of Hitler and Mussolini in Europe and Africa, and that the Axis strategists considered the world as one gigantic battlefield. To prove his propositions the President reminded his hearers that in 1931 Japan invaded Manchukuo; that in 1935 Italy invaded Ethiopia; that in 1938 Hitler occupied Austria; that in 1939 Hitler invaded Czechoslovakia and Poland; that in 1940 Hitler invaded Norway, Denmark, the Netherlands, Belgium, and Luxembourg; that in the same year Italy attacked France and Greece; and that in 1941 the Axis Powers attacked Yugoslavia and Greece and dominated the Balkans, Hitler invaded Russia, and Japan attacked Malaya, Thailand, and the United States.

Evidence of documents may appear in many forms, among which are birth certificates, marriage licenses, deeds, receipts of sales, and literary publications. For example, in an address to the American Society of International Law, on April 23, 1965, Dean Rusk introduced as evidence an editorial from *Pravda*. On May 15, 1965, at a National Teach-in on Vietnam, in Washington, D.C., Professor Robert A. Scalapino introduced an editorial from *The Peking Daily Worker.* On January 29, 1964, the Government of Vietnam submitted to the International Control Commission a list of weapons and other military equipment that had been captured from the Vietcong. The use of published materials is a common form of documentation.

Evidence of pictorializations may appear through charts, sketches, diagrams, and photographs. This type of evidence recently appeared at a church service in which the speaker introduced pictures that he took in India. The clergyman used the pictures to convince hearers that the Indians need food and medical attention to survive. Other recent examples of this type of evidence are the pictures of the moon that the astronauts took during the Apollo missions.

Recent mechanical improvements in recording devices have prompted some clergymen to introduce as evidence tape recordings and videotape recordings. For example, a clergyman recently introduced to his hearers tape recordings he had made while interviewing over three hundred Negroes in Milwaukee. The clergyman used the recordings to prove to his audience that not all of the Milwaukee Negroes are in agreement with the actions of the Reverend James Groppi. Another clergyman introduced to his hearers a videotape recording he had made of a discussion by high-school students about the 1968 Presidential race. He used the recording to prove that high-school students are well informed on American issues and thus should have the right to vote.

Evidence of relics also appears in many forms. For example, the evidence may appear as rocks and minerals in a lecture on geology; as soil in a discussion on agriculture or conservation; or as knives, guns, poisons, dentures, fingerprints, footprints, blood samples, human hairs, paint, and clothing in cases of homicide. In general, a relic is anything meeting the definition of evidence which is not testimony from witnesses, testimony in written form, historical facts, documents, pictorializations, and recordings.

Too frequently speakers attempt to awe their hearers by introducing a plethora of evidence. There is nothing wrong with having at hand a large quantity of evidence, as long as all of the evidence is *clear, accurate,* and *reliable.* The clergy would be wise to abide by the following criteria for evaluating the quality of evidence.

One question the speaker should ask is: "If my witness is a lay witness, does he report only his observations?" A lay witness is a person who is not trained to observe a particular event. Such witnesses often are called upon to testify on the events of an occurrence in question. Even though such a person is not an expert or trained observer, what he reports can be taken as factual. As long as he reports only what he observed and not his opinions or inferences, his testimony is factual in nature. A "No" answer to the first question is reason to dismiss the witness.

A second question to ask is: "Is my witness physically reliable?" To be physically reliable a witness must have been near enough to the scene to observe it fully and clearly, and must possess the sensory instruments needed for accurate observation of the occurrence. For example, how can a deaf person who is unable to read lips testify to what was said between two or more persons? How can a blind person testify to the fact that a driver went through a stop sign? A "No" reply to the second major question is reason to dismiss the witness.

A third question to ask is: "Is my witness biased toward the subject?" A biased person tends to close his eyes to evidence alleged against something in which he believes. He attempts to deduce facts from principles, rather than principles from facts. That is, he reasons *a priori*, "in advance" of the facts. He tends to assume a dichotomy where no such simplification is justified. He refuses to accept the possibility of a middle ground; to him everything is either all good or all bad. A biased person also is one who receives money or other compensation for what he says. Whenever a person stands to profit from what he may say, such a person should be dismissed as a witness.

A fourth question is: "Is my witness evading the issue?" There are numerous ways to evade an issue. For example, one may interject humor, sarcasm, or parody. Clemenceau is alleged to have remarked, "Fourteen points; fourteen points! Why the Lord Almighty had only ten!" Clemenceau's quip may have been humorous, but it evaded the merits of President Wilson's plan. A person may also evade the issue by attacking a person's character, race, or religion, instead of dealing with the person's contentions. This fallacy is called *argumentum ad hominem*. Another way to evade the issue is to point to another wrong. For illustration, a particular minister in a speech class performed poorly. After the instructor had finished his criticism of the minister's performance, the minister replied, "Well, the other members of the class didn't do well either." The fact that the other students performed poorly was irrelevant to the main issue, namely, the minister's poor performance. Still another way to evade an issue is to call the subject "trite," "irrelevant," or "unnecessary," and to employ such phrases as "I don't have to explain to an intelligent group like you," and "As anyone can see." People who evade discussion and argument usually make poor witnesses.

A fifth question to ask is: "Is the testimony of my witness consistent with itself and with the laws of argument?" People who contradict themselves in different situations or under cross-examination, or who employ arguments that momentarily sound well and catch the audience off guard, but under careful analysis prove to be fallacious, usually contribute little to credibility. A "No" answer to the above question is reason to dismiss the witness.

A sixth question to ask is: "Is my witness compatible with other reliable evidence?" Many people are careless when reporting. One clergyman in a speech class constantly was inaccurate in citing dates of significant historical events. Another clergyman frequently overlooked significant factors which, if introduced, would have changed the complexion of his argument. For example, in one of his speeches the clergyman contended that a particular curve in a certain road in his hometown should be altered because twelve people were killed in traffic accidents on that curve. However, another clergyman from the same town offered evidence that revealed that eight of the twelve fatalities occurred in a head-on crash by two cars, and that both of the drivers had been under the influence of alcohol; that two other persons were killed because of a blowout in an old tire; and that another person was killed because he had been driving too fast for road conditions. Hence, at least eleven of the twelve deaths occurred through reasons other than the curve in the road. Quoting out of context is another form of carelessness. For example, several clergymen in a speech class omitted certain portions of quotations so that meanings not intended by the original sources were conveyed. In each situation reliable evidence contradicted the clergymen, and in each situation the clergyman guilty of the fallacy became extremely embarrassed. Such inaccurate witnesses must be dismissed.

A seventh question is: "Does my evidence adhere to the rules for definition?" Definitions are intended to show how something works, what something does, how something has originated and developed, or how something compares or contrasts with something else. The clergy should make certain that the definitions in their evidence treat the characteristics properly included in the subject; exclude everything not properly included in the subject; clarify the concepts without depending upon the terms themselves or their derivatives; and possess immediate intelligibility value. Any violation of these criteria is reason to dismiss the evidence.

An eighth question to ask is: "Does my evidence represent the latest data on the subject?" Evidence that is behind the times lacks *ethos,* and usually is rejected by those members of the audience who are well informed on the subject at hand.

A ninth question is: "Are my source materials authentic?" Copies of documents, pictures, and recordings can be changed through error or through premeditated editing. Therefore, it is necessary that the speaker knows whether his evidence is authentic or forged. The speaker should at least attempt to ascertain the authorship of the source, and establish the time and place of origin of the source. Authenticity of authorship may be verified by direct evidence in the forms of statements recorded in the author's diary or letters, or by comparing the style, penmanship, and general tone of the alleged evidence with other works known to be by the same author. The time and place of origin of the source may be established by the headings on the documents, by the watermarks on the paper, by references to events known to have occurred at a particular time, or even by a carbon 14 test to detect the age of the paper.

Finally, the speaker should ask himself: "Can the literal and the real meanings of my evidence be established?" Literal meanings may be understood by carefully analyzing words or phrases that are foreign, archaic, or technical. Real meanings may be established by analyzing ambiguities and figurative language, and by viewing all of the work in context. A "No" reply to the above question is reason to dismiss the evidence.

In conclusion, this section on evidence does not allege to exhaust all of the ways by which a speaker may evaluate the quality of his evidence. Instead, this section recommends certain tests that all members of the clergy should be able to perform so as to make the evidence acceptable to the hearers. The thesis of this section is that evidence of low credibility usually fails to generate persuasion.

Formal mental processes must be used by the speaker to weave the major concepts and evidence into a complete and meaningful pattern. The inductive and deductive processes are the cohesive forces. By establishing certain relationships, the processes guide the audience from the recognition of the discernible facts to certain conclusions.

Ideally, all public speakers should study formal treatises on logic, but many preachers are too busy to read, let alone to study intensively such literature. Therefore, invalid inductive and deductive processes probably are the most typical discrepancies that appear in the pulpit. The purpose of this section is to acquaint the reader with certain fundamental principles of logic, and to encourage the reader to study formal treatises on logic in order to improve communicative effectiveness.

Before introducing the fundamental principles of logic, certain definitions are warranted.

"Validity" refers to the nature of relationships between propositions, rather than to the truth of propositions. A mental process is valid when the conclusion is forced by the premises.

The "truth" of a proposition means that the proposition coordinates with the facts to which it refers.

The "falsity" of a proposition means that the proposition fails to coordinate with the facts to which it refers.

A "sound" argument consists of true propositions and a valid relationship between the premises and the conclusions.

1. *Inductive processes.* These proceed from the specific to the general, inferring that what is true of some members of a given class is true of all members of that class. Such processes involve extensions of fact into the unknown or unproved. The "leap" from the known to the unknown is based on the assumption that certain relationships are invariant and recurrent throughout the universe. The speaker assumes that because of the uniformity and regularity of his evidence, the principles

thought to be true in the past continue to be true in the future. Inductive processes occur through examples, analogies, and causal relations.

a. An induction through examples appeared in President Roosevelt's address to the American people on the evening of December 8, 1941. In this speech the President informed his hearers that the Axis Powers invaded, attacked, and occupied many countries without warning. Because of the uniformity of his evidence, the President made an inductive leap and inferred that the Axis Powers were using one pattern to conquer the world. This induction may be seen more clearly in the following diagram.

INDUCTION THROUGH EXAMPLE

1. RELIANCE ON EVIDENCE OF HISTORICAL FACTS:	→	2. UNIFORMITY AND REGULARITY OF THE EVIDENCE:	→	3. THE INDUCTIVE LEAP BASED ON THE UNIFORMITY AND REGULARITY OF THE EVIDENCE
a. Manchukuo b. Ethiopia c. Austria d. Czechoslovakia e. Poland f. Norway g. Denmark h. Netherlands i. Belgium j. Luxembourg k. France l. Greece m. Yugoslavia n. Balkan States o. Russia p. Malaya q. Thailand r. United States		a. All of the countries alluded to were attacked, occupied, or invaded by the Axis Powers. b. All of the countries alluded to were attacked, occupied, or invaded without warning.		↓ 4. THE INFERENCE RESULTING FROM STEPS 1, 2, AND 3: ∴ The Axis Powers are using one pattern to conquer the world.

President Roosevelt's inductive process is logically sound for several reasons. First, the examples are historically accurate. Second, the examples are uniform; that is, they belong in the class or form of experience that they were intended to exemplify. Third, the President introduced a sufficient number of examples to protect himself from committing the fallacy of hasty generalization. In other words, the President did not base his conclusion on an insufficient quantity of evidence. Fourth, the examples account for many different circumstances. By showing a cross section of the countries attacked by the Axis Powers, President Roosevelt made it difficult for anyone to label his inference as an unrepresentative generalization. Such a fallacy occurs when the examples fail to enjoy a representative dispersion. (For example, a clergyman once polled over four thousand Roman Catholics in a particularly large midwestern city, and concluded that Roman Catholics in the United States generally favor the war in Vietnam. By having an extensive acquaintance with specific examples, the clergyman did not make a hasty generalization. But by limiting his poll to one midwestern city, the clergyman did not earn the right to predict with any assurance the beliefs of Roman Catholics on a nationwide basis.) Finally, the President presented his examples in sufficient detail so as to make them immediately intelligible to his hearers. The clergy would be wise to practice the above procedures when establishing their inductions through example, for any violation of the preceding criteria makes the induction logically unsound.

b. When employing inductive processes through analogy, the speaker assumes that what is true of one set of phenomena may be true of another set of phenomena, because the two sets have certain formal characteristics in common. From the known structure of one set of phenomena the speaker infers knowledge concerning some unknown portion of the second set. The basis for inference is that the structure of the second set is the same as the structure of the first set and consequently invariant relations which are manifested in the first will also be manifested in the second.

For example, at a dinner of the Chamber of Commerce of the State of New York, in New York City, May 8, 1883, Henry Ward Beecher contended that men are analogous to timber, for

> Oak will bear a stress that pine won't, but there never was a stick of timber on the earth that could not be broken at some pressure. There never was a man born on the earth that could not be broken at some pressure — not always the same nor put in the same place. There is many a man who cannot be broken by money pressure, but who can be by pressure of flattery. There is many a man impervious to flattery who is warped and biased by his social inclinations. There is many a man whom you cannot tempt with red gold, but you can with dinners and convivialities. One way or the other, every man is vincible.[1]

When speaking on "The Form of Godliness Without Its Power," William Chillingworth said:

> For, as the shadows are longest when the sun is lowest, and as vines and other fruit-trees bear the less fruit when they are suffered to luxuriate and spend their sap upon superfluous suckers, and abundance of leaves; so, commonly, we may observe, both in civil conservation, where there is great store of formality, there is little sincerity; and in religion, where there is decay of true cordial piety, there men entertain and please themselves, and vainly hope to please God, with external formalities and performances.[2]

In his sermon on "Jesus' Ethical Message Confronts the World," Dr. Harry Emerson Fosdick said that

> The most shameful aspect of our present international situation, I think, is the way we ape the enemies we hate. The dictatorships say, War! so we say, War! They build vast armaments, so we build vast armaments. Step by step, day by day, we become their yes-men. They say, Dictatorial control of the nation for the sake of war's efficiency! So in Washington we propose bills that provide on the day of war's declaration that the nation shall conscript life, property, labor, conscience. The dictatorships say, Let the War Department determine the foreign policy! So we, too, against the tradition of our people and the very words of our Constitution, say the same thing, and in Washington — witness the proposition for the fortification of Guam — not so much the civilian representatives of the people as the army and the navy begin to initiate, and so ultimately to predetermine, our foreign policy. What apes we are![3]

Since the strength of an analogy depends upon the similarity of structure between two sets of phenomena, the speaker must make certain that there is no profound difference between his analogous phenomena, and that there are a sufficient number of fundamental points of similarity between the phenomena. If these two corollaries are ignored, chances are that the analogy will be superficial and the argument will be nonpersuasive.

c. The nature of causal relations has long been a matter of dispute among theologians, philosophers, and scientists. This section is not intended to present an extended history of this dispute, but rather to recommend certain basic tests which should help the preacher to evaluate the strengths and weaknesses of arguments alleged to be causally related.

The first test is to make certain that coincidence, or an isolated example of sequence, has not been mistaken for regularity. Failure to consider this possibility often results in the fallacy of *post hoc ergo propter hoc*, a Latin phrase meaning, "after this therefore because of this." This phrase is an elliptical way of saying, "That event came after this event; hence that event came because of this event." For instance, suppose that at 7:30 A.M., a black cat crossed the path of Mr. Jones. At 7:45 A.M., while climbing the stairs to his office, Mr. Jones tripped and sprained his ankle. His first reply was, "That blasted cat; I knew something like this would happen!" Obviously the cat had nothing to do with Mr. Jones' misfortune. Yet Mr. Jones quickly established a causal relation. Members of the clergy who mistake coincidence for regularity open themselves to attack by cross-examination.

The second test is to make certain that regularity has not been mistaken for either cause or effect. For example, suppose that on four occasions Mr. Sutherland went golfing with Mr. Roberts, and that on each occasion the men were caught in a thunderstorm. After the last incident, Mr. Sutherland informed his wife that he never again would play golf with Mr. Roberts because the latter "is nothing but a jinx." Little wonder that Mrs. Sutherland laughed at her husband's remark. Certainly Mr. Roberts had nothing to do with bringing about the thunderstorms. Yet Mr. Sutherland established a causal relation. Clergymen who mistake regularity for either cause or effect also may be laughed at by their hearers.

The third test is to make certain that a necessary factor has not been confused with a sufficient factor, or that the alleged cause is sufficient to produce the alleged effect. People often fail to observe that a causal factor may be necessary but by itself insufficient to produce a given effect. As an illustration, the assassination of the Archduke Francis Ferdinand and his wife at Sarajevo, Bosnia, may have immediately caused hostilities, but history reveals that the assassination was not the primary cause of World War I. However, there are people today who still contend that the assassination of the Archduke was *the* cause of the war. Such causal relations should be abandoned by the clergy.

The final test is to make certain that other relevant factors have not been overlooked which could obstruct or prevent the alleged cause from operating to produce the alleged effect. For example, some people predicted that when World War II ended, the unemployment resulting from factories which stopped producing war goods would lead to an economic depression in the United States. However, such people failed to consider such intervening factors as shortages of consumer goods created during the war, an extreme demand for United States goods by other countries, an expanding population, and the Marshall Plan and Point Four Program. To overlook relevant factors when establishing causal relations is not conducive to effective communication.

In conclusion, clergymen who want to improve their communicative effectiveness should select and utilize only those inductive processes that pass the tests recommended above.

2. *Deductive processes.* These proceed from a general truth to a particular conclusion. Each deductive process is an organization of three propositions, consisting of a major premise, a minor premise, and a conclusion. When all three propositions appear, then the deductive process is a *syllogism.* When one of the premises or the conclusion is suppressed, then the deductive process is an *enthymeme.* Consider the following examples.

(1) All wealthy nations should help the poor.
The United States is a wealthy nation.
Therefore, the United States should help the poor.

(2) All wealthy nations should help the poor, and
The United States is a wealthy nation.

(3) All wealthy nations should help the poor, and
The United States should help the poor.

(4) The United States should help the poor, because
The United States is a wealthy nation.

In the first example, all three propositions appear. The major premise is: "All wealthy nations should help the poor." The minor premise is: "The United States is a wealthy nation." The conclusion is: "Therefore, the United States should help the poor." Hence, example 1 is a syllogism.

The other examples are enthymemes. Example 2 is an enthymeme because the conclusion is suppressed. Example 3 is an enthymeme because the minor premise is suppressed. And example 4 is an enthymeme because the major premise is suppressed. With this information in mind, an examination of the different types of proposition and the basic rules that govern the validity of deductive processes is now warranted.

3. *Types of proposition.* Preachers should acquaint themselves with four types of proposition: categorical, hypothetical, alternative, and disjunctive.

a. The *categorical proposition* asserts, defines, or classifies without qualification. That is, the categorical proposition asserts without any condition, alternative, or sign of incompatibility. The sign of assertion is the present tense of the verb "to be," namely "am," "is," or "are." The verb is called the "copula." Although the verbs are of the present tense, in the logical function of language they have no reference to time. Any temporal significance is expressed in the predicate term. By "term" we mean any word or group of words that functions as the subject or predicate of a proposition. For example, while we normally would say, "College students should employ grammatically correct language," the speaker, in order to keep the sign of assertion logically pure, should say, "College students are people who should employ grammatically correct language." Of course, elliptical statements are permissible so long as one understands the correct logical formulation.

Categorical propositions are defined by their "quality" and "quantity." The quality of a proposition is either "affirmative" or "negative." The quantity of a proposition is determined by the subject term alone. If the entire denotation of the subject term is referred to in the proposition, then the proposition is "universal." If only part of the subject term is referred to in the proposition, then the proposition is "particular" in quantity. Categorical propositions may be (1) affirmative and universal, (2) affirmative and particular, (3) negative and universal, and (4) negative and particular. Such propositions respectively are called "A," "I," "E," and "O" categorical propositions.

Affirmative and universal ("A") propositions assert that the entire denotation of the subject term is included in the predicate class. Universal propositions may be divided into a "general" class or a "singular" class.

General propositions are those whose subject term is either a general name or an indefinite description. Examples are: "All philosophers are seekers of truth," and "All professional soldiers are lovers of adventure." In the first example the subject term, "philosophers," is a general name, whereas in the second example the subject term, "professional soldiers," is an indefinite description. In both examples the subject term is indefinite in denotation; no individual is singled out.

General "A" propositions usually are introduced by such words as "all," "every," or "any." Examples are: "All of these books are priceless"; "Every book is priceless"; and "Any book is priceless."

The definite article "the" and the indefinite article "a" sometimes are used in the sense of "all." To illustrate: "The elephant is a quadruped" means "All elephants are quadrupeds." "A man is a two-legged creature" means that "All men are two-legged creatures." Sometimes "all" is to be understood, though not verbally expressed. For example, "War is atrocious" means "All wars are atrocious."

Singular propositions are those whose subject term is definite in denotation. Singular universal affirmative propositions may occur several ways. The subject term may be a proper name as in "Harry Emerson Fosdick is one of the world's foremost preachers." The subject term may be a personal pronoun as in "He (She, It) is intelligent"; or "We (You, They) are industrious." The subject term may be a definite description as in "The fastest human in the world is an American athlete." Or the subject term may have numerical definite singularity as in "The last three golf courses beside this highway are newly built and privately owned and operated." These examples are "universal" because the entire denotation of the subject term is referred to in the propositions. They are "singular" because the subject term is definite in denotation. They are "affirmative" because, after the terms are set aside, the remaining portion of the propositions reveals no negation by such words as "no" or "not."

Affirmative and particular ("I") propositions assert that less than the entire denotation of the subject term is referred to in the proposition. To state the same idea in another way, "I" propositions assert that only part of the class of individuals denoted by the subject term is included in the predicate class. The expression of quantity may vary in vagueness because of such phrases as "some are," "few are," "many are," "most are," "several are," "nearly all are," and "all but a few are." On other occasions the expression of quantity may be more precise because of numerical indications as "10 percent are," "only five of the group are," and "all but fifty are." Preachers should eliminate vagueness whenever possible.

Negative and universal ("E") propositions assert that the entire denotation of the subject term is excluded from the predicate class. General "E" propositions are formed by introducing the negative sign "No" in the beginning of the subject term. For example, "No professional American athletes are able to perform in the Olympic Games." The "No" actually performs double duty. It makes clear that the entire denotation of the subject term is referred to, and it serves as the negative sign. Singular "E" propositions are formed simply by introducing the negative sign "not" into connection with the copula. For example, "The fastest human in the world is not an American athlete."

Negative and particular ("O") propositions assert that at least part of the subject class is excluded from the predicate class. "O" propositions are formed by introducing the negative sign "not" with the copula. For example, "Some students are not good examples of character."

b. The *hypothetical proposition* expresses condition or implication. It contains two member propositions, the first proposition being the "antecedent," and the second proposition being the "consequent." The antecedent usually begins with the word "if," and the consequent with the word "then." The conjunction of these words and the words "were," "would," or "should" indicates the hypothetical nature of the proposition. The hypothetical proposition as a whole implies *the relation* of the antecedent to the consequent, and makes no claim to the truth of either the antecedent or the consequent. For instance, while defending Tom Paine, Thomas Erskine stated:

> If I were to ask you, Gentlemen of the jury, what is the choicest fruit that grows upon the tree of English liberty, you would answer: SECURITY UNDER THE LAW. If I were to ask the whole people of England the return they looked for at the hands of Government for the burdens under which they bend to support it, I should still be answered: SECURITY UNDER THE LAW; or, in other words, an impartial administration of justice.[4]

For further illustration, on April 27, 1898, Albert J. Beveridge said to the Middlesex Club of Boston:

> If this means the Stars and Stripes over an Isthmian canal, over Hawaii, over Cuba, and the southern seas, . . . then let us meet that meaning with a mighty joy and make that meaning good, no matter what barbarism and all our foes may say or do.[5]

c. The *alternative proposition* contains two or more component propositions. The first component begins with the word "either," and the following components with the word "or." The alternative proposition claims that its member propositions exhaust the relevant possibilities, that at least one of the alternants is true, and that no proposition outside the true proposition need be considered. However, the alternative proposition fails to state clearly which alternative is true. In fact, it fails to preclude that all possibilities are true. For example, in his speech delivered in Springfield, on June 16, 1858, Abraham Lincoln stated:

> either the *opponents* of slavery, will arrest the further spread of it, and place it where the public mind shall rest in the belief that it is in the course of ultimate extinction; or its *advocates* will push it forward till it shall become alike unlawful in *all* the states, *old* as well as *new* — *North* as well as *South*.[6]

d. The *disjunctive proposition* expresses incompatibility. This type of proposition contains two member propositions called "disjuncts." The first disjunct usually begins with the words "not both" or "it cannot both be"; whereas the second disjunct begins with "and." The disjunctive proposition asserts that not both of the disjuncts can be true. However, the proposition fails to claim that either disjunct is true, for neither disjunct may be warranted by the evidence. In other words, the disjunctive proposition asserts that not both of its disjuncts can be true, but both disjuncts may be false. Thus, a speaker might argue, "Not both can the President be in the United States and in France." (More commonly, "The President cannot be both in the United States and in France.") If the evidence were to prove that the President is in the United States, then it would be false to say that he is in France. If the evidence were to prove that he is in France, then it would be false to say that he is in the United States. Not both disjuncts can be true. However, evidence might prove that the President is in England. Then both of the above disjuncts would be false.

4. *Testing the validity of deduction.* Although most of the deductive processes employed in daily life appear enthymematically — that is, syllogistically, but with one of the premises or the conclusion suppressed — the validity or invalidity of deductive processes appears more clearly in complete syllogistic form. Hence, it would be wise for preachers to prepare their sermons by casting their deductive processes in complete syllogistic form and then applying tests to determine the validity of their deductions. The following basic rules should help them to improve their communicative effectiveness. If time permits, they should expand their knowledge of logic by reading formal treatises on logic.

a. *Categorical syllogisms.* The first rule is that *every syllogism must contain three propositions and three terms and only three propositions and three terms.* Consider the following syllogism:

All human beings are creatures of God.
John is a human being.
Therefore, John is a creature of God.

The first proposition is the major premise. The second proposition is the minor premise. The third proposition is the conclusion. To say it differently, "John," the subject term of the conclusion, is the minor term; and the proposition that contains the minor term is the minor premise. "Is a creature of God," the predicate term of the conclusion, is the major term; and the proposition that contains the major term is the major premise. The term to which the major and minor terms are related in the major and minor premises is the middle term, and the middle term appears in both premises. Therefore, "human being" is the middle term.

From the above relationship one can draw a valid conclusion. But suppose that a categorical syllogism were to contain more than three terms. For example, what definite conclusion can result from the following relationship?

All human beings are creatures of God.
John is a brilliant scholar and athlete.
Therefore, ____________________.

Indeed, no conclusion can occur from the above relationship.

The second rule is that *the middle term must be distributed at least once.* A term is distributed when its entire denotation is referred to in the proposition. Only universal propositions distribute their subjects, and only negative propositions distribute their predicates. In the following examples the distributed portions are italicized: "All *human beings* are creatures of God." "No *human being* is *a creature of God.*" "Some human beings are not *creatures of God.*" "Some human beings are creatures of God." The first example is a universal proposition distributing its subject. The second is a universal proposition distributing its subject, and a negative proposition distributing its predicate. The third statement is a negative proposition distributing its predicate. No distribution appears in the final example, because the proposition is neither universal nor negative. If the speaker fails to distribute the middle term at least once, then his audience has no way of telling whether the minor term and major term are related to the middle term. When the major and minor terms have no common ground, no logical conclusion can result.

The third rule is that *no term may be distributed in the conclusion when the term is undistributed in its premise.* If the speaker distributes the minor term in the conclusion, but not in the minor premise, then he commits the fallacy of the illicit process of the minor. If the speaker distributes the major term in the conclusion, but not in the major premise, then he commits the fallacy of the illicit process of the major. In either case, the speaker asserts more in the conclusion than the premises allow. Consider the following syllogisms:

> No true Christian is a friend of the Devil.
> All friends of the Devil are people heading for disaster.
> Therefore, no person heading for disaster is a true Christian.

> All good citizens are voters on election day.
> Some people are not good citizens.
> Therefore, some people are not voters on election day.

In the first syllogism the minor term functions with a broader extension in the conclusion than in the minor premise. Therefore, the first syllogism is a fallacy of the illicit process of the minor. In the second syllogism more is said about the major term in the conclusion than in the major premise. Therefore, the second syllogism is a fallacy of the illicit process of the major.

The fourth rule is that *nothing can be inferred from two negative premises.* By excluding the major term from the middle term, and the minor term from the middle term, the speaker prevents his hearers from relating the minor term to the major term.

The fifth rule is that *if one of the premises is negative, the conclusion must be negative; and that to prove a negative conclusion, one of the premises must be negative.*

> No true Christian is a friend of the Devil.
> All converts are true Christians.
> Therefore, no converts are friends of the Devil.

The sixth rule is that *no conclusion can be drawn from two particular premises.* A combination of two negative particular premises commits the fallacy of drawing a conclusion from two negative premises. A combination of two affirmative particular premises commits the fallacy of the undistributed middle term. A combination of an affirmative particular major premise and a negative particular minor premise commits the fallacy of the illicit process of the major. And the combination of a negative particular major premise and an affirmative particular minor premise commits the fallacy of the illicit process of the major, or the fallacy of the undistributed middle term.

The seventh rule is that *if one premise is particular, then the conclusion must be particular.* The combination of two negative premises commits the fallacy of drawing a conclusion from two negative premises. In the combination of two affirmative propositions such as "A-I," the conclusion would have to be particular, or it would be universal affirmative or negative. If universal affirmative, the fallacy of the illicit process of the minor would result. If universal negative, a violation of the fifth rule would result. In the combination of two affirmative propositions such as "I-A," if the conclusion were universal affirmative, either the fallacy of the illicit process of the minor or that of the undistributed middle term would result, depending on the location of the middle term in the premises. If the conclusion were universal negative, then rule five again would be violated.

In the combination of one affirmative and one negative proposition, if the conclusion were affirmative, then rule five would be violated. If the conclusion were universal negative, the following fallacies would occur. An "A-O" combination would produce either the undistributed middle term or the illicit process of the major or the minor. An "E-I" combination would produce the illicit process of the minor. An "O-A" combination would bring about either the undistributed middle term or the illicit process of the major or minor, and an "I-E" combination would produce the illicit process of the major.

The final rule is that *no conclusion can be drawn from a particular major premise and a negative minor premise.* If any conclusion were attempted, it would have to be negative because of rule five. In such a case the major term would then be distributed. However, since nothing can be inferred from two negative premises, the major premise would have to be affirmative. Being particular affirmative, the major term would then be undistributed. Hence, the attempted conclusion would result in the illicit process of the major.

b. *Hypothetical syllogisms.* The hypothetical proposition claims that the truth of the consequent would follow from the truth of the antecedent and that the falsity of the antecedent would follow from the falsity of the consequent. The hypothetical proposition merely asserts that its antecedent is one logical condition of the truth of the consequent. Whether there are other logical conditions of the truth of the consequent is not asserted. Therefore, the rejection of the stated condition does not warrant the rejection of the consequent. Nor does the acceptance of the truth of the consequent justify the acceptance of the one condition expressed in the antecedent.

In the light of the above explanation, the speaker has two ways to develop the hypothetical syllogism. In the first, *when the minor premise affirms the antecedent, then the conclusion must affirm the consequent,* as in the following:

> If we continue to spend money foolishly, then we will lose our wealth.
> We will continue to spend money foolishly.
> Therefore, we will lose our wealth.

In the second form of the hypothetical syllogism, *when the minor premise denies the consequent, then the conclusion must deny the antecedent:*

> If we continue to spend money foolishly, then we will lose our wealth.
> We will not lose our wealth.
> Therefore, we will not continue to spend money foolishly.

These are the only valid ways to develop the hypothetical syllogism!

c. *Alternative syllogisms.* The alternative syllogism has for its major premise an alternative proposition that asserts that at least one of its alternants is true, and perhaps both are true. Since the possibility of their both being true is open, the affirmation of one of the alternants in the minor premise warrants no definite conclusion with respect to the other alternant. However, if the speaker were to deny one of the alternants in the minor premise, then he validly could affirm the other alternant in the conclusion. Hence, the speaker must develop alternative syllogisms *by eliminating in the minor premise all alternants except the one to be affirmed in the conclusion.*

An example of a valid alternative syllogism is:

> Either we will go to the football game, or we will have a party.
> We will not have a party.
> Therefore, we will go to the football game.

An example of an invalid alternative syllogism is:

> Either we will go to the football game, or we will have a party.
> We will have a party.
> Therefore, we will [will not] go to the football game.

d. *Disjunctive syllogisms.* The disjunctive proposition asserts that not both of its member propositions can be true, but both can be false. No valid conclusion can occur when the minor premise denies one of the disjuncts of the major premise. The speaker must *affirm one of the disjuncts in the minor premise, and must deny the remaining disjunct in the conclusion.* The reader should note that the development of the disjunctive syllogism is opposite to the development of the alternative syllogism. In the minor premise the disjunctive syllogism affirms, whereas the alternative syllogism denies. In the conclusion the disjunctive syllogism denies, whereas the alternative syllogism affirms.

An example of a valid disjunctive syllogism is:

> Not both can we go to the football game and have a party.
> We will have a party.
> Therefore, we will not go to the football game.

5. *The dilemma.* Before concluding an examination of certain basic principles of deduction, a brief look at the dilemma is warranted. The dilemma is compound syllogistic reasoning. The major premise contains two hypothetical propositions, and the minor premise is an alternative proposition. To develop the dilemma, the speaker must follow the rules for hypothetical reasoning. *Either the minor premise must affirm the antecedents, and then the conclusion must affirm the consequents; or the minor premise must deny the consequents, and then the conclusion must deny the antecedents.*

If the antecedent of the first hypothetical proposition is identical to the antecedent of the second proposition, or if the consequents are identical, then the dilemma is "simple" in quality. If the propositions have different consequents and antecedents, then the dilemma is "complex" in quality. A "constructive" dilemma affirms the antecedents and then affirms the consequents. A "destructive" dilemma denies the consequents and then denies the antecedents. The following examples illustrate the different types of dilemma:

a. *The Simple Constructive Dilemma:*

If we win first place, then we should be pleased; and if we win second place, then we should be pleased.

Either we will win first place, or we will win second place.

Therefore, we should be pleased.

b. *The Simple Destructive Dilemma:*

If we elect a new leader, then we will have more duties to perform; and if we elect a new leader, then we will have to pay higher dues.

Either we will not have more duties to perform, or we will not have to pay higher dues.

Therefore, we will not elect a new leader.

c. *The Complex Constructive Dilemma:*

If we continue to fight in Vietnam, then we must cut back on our welfare programs; and if we discontinue to fight in Vietnam, then we will displease our Vietnamese allies.

Either we will continue to fight in Vietnam, or we will discontinue to fight in Vietnam.

Therefore, either we must cut back on our welfare programs, or we will displease our Vietnamese allies.

d. *The Complex Destructive Dilemma:*

If this man were honest, then he would not cheat on his tax returns; and if this man were educated properly, then he would not use poor grammar.

Either this man cheats on his tax returns, or he uses poor grammar.

Therefore, either this man is not honest, or he is not educated properly.

When faced with a dilemma, the speaker may attempt to combat it by one or more methods. First, prove that the premises are false. Second, prove that the major premise has failed to exhaust all of the possibilities. Third, show that the structure is invalid. In other words, prove that the opposition either has denied the antecedent and then attempted to draw a conclusion, or that he has affirmed the consequent before drawing his conclusion. Fourth, propose a counterdilemma; prove that another conclusion denies the conclusion of the opponent. Finally, "turn the tables" on the opponent. Use the opponent's dilemma but prove that his conclusion works against him rather than for him.

In conclusion, deductive processes are potential generators of persuasion, but preachers should employ only those processes that meet the preceding tests of validity.

PATHOS

Charles Henry Woolbert, one of the founders of the modern speech profession, once remarked that "to study Persuasion intensively is to study human nature minutely. . . . More than half of success in winning men is in understanding how they work."[7] In other words, persuasion is dependent upon motivation.

Ideally, students of persuasion should study the works of rhetoricians and psychologists who specialize in the explanation of personality and human motives. However, preachers often lack the time to read, let alone to study intensively the numerous and often complicated psychological treatises. One significant result is that many preachers appear to lack understanding of the forces that impel human beings to act. The following material is designed to remedy this liability. However, the authors wish to encourage the clergy to read formal treatises on motivation as supplements to this work.

At least three steps are necessary when preparing one's *pathos*. First, the speaker should determine the appropriate motivational situations — that is, situations in which people are moved to act. Second, the speaker should select the general *topoi* or lines of argument he wishes to employ. Finally, the speaker should select only those specific emotional appeals that coordinate with the general *topoi*. Specific emotional appeals are those modes of persuasion that arouse in an audience a sense of anger, contempt, calmness, friendship, loyalty, pride, duty, fear, confidence, shame, shamelessness, kindness, indignation, envy, emulation, etc.

Encouraged by such works as John Dashiell's *Fundamentals of General Psychology*, Aristotle's *Rhetoric*, and Spinoza's *The Ethics*, Professor Otis M. Walter established five basic motivational situations: the *difficulty situation*, the *goal-oriented situation*, the *barrier situation*, the *threat situation*, and the *identification situation*.[8]

The *difficulty situation* arises when "an individual or group of individuals perceives a difficulty." That is, the audience feels, vaguely or clearly, that something is wrong. Walter considers this motivational situation as the most fundamental situation. John Dewey, for example, contended "that no man ever thinks unless he is first confronted with a felt difficulty." The *goal-oriented situation* "arises when individuals are considering certain rather well-defined goals as solutions to a difficulty." The *barrier situation* arises when well-defined goals become complicated by a barrier between the goals and the people who want to achieve the goals. The *threat situation* arises when people are moved to action because of a threat that will harm them or their immediate loved ones or friends. The *identification situation* "arises when human beings act for the benefit of other groups." [9]

Once the speaker has determined the appropriate motivational situations, he next should select the general *topoi* or lines of argument he wishes to employ in each motivational situation. For example, in the *difficulty situation* the speaker might argue that there is no difficulty; that there is a difficulty, but that it is easy to overcome; that the audience must attempt to define the difficulty; that to attack the difficulty is futile or, perhaps, even fatal; or that the audience should deal with other difficulties that are more important and demanding. In the *goal-oriented situation* the speaker might argue, for example, that the audience should achieve a certain goal, or that they should abandon a certain goal. In the *barrier situation* the speaker might argue, for example, that the audience should achieve the goal, despite the barrier; that the audience should work toward a substitute goal; or that the audience should study ways of eradicating or reducing the barrier. In the *threat situation* the speaker might urge the audience to give up the goal, to resist and combat the threat, or to forget the threat because it is not strong enough to warrant their attention. Finally in the *identification situation* the speaker might argue that the audience should help a particular group, or that the audience should not help the group.

Once the speaker has determined his general lines of argument, he next should select those specific emotional appeals that coordinate with the general *topoi.* Thus, in the *difficulty situation* the speaker might argue that the difficulty is unjust, irrational, or unworthy, thus appealing to the audience's sense of contempt or anger. In the *goal-oriented situation* the speaker might argue that his audience should achieve a certain goal. Within such a general *topoi,* the speaker might appeal to his audience's sense of calmness and pride by arguing that the desired goal will bring pleasure, wealth, plenty of friends, security, and prestige. In the *barrier situation* the speaker might argue that the audience should achieve the goal despite the barrier. Within such a general *topoi,* the speaker might appeal to the audience's sense of anger or hatred by arguing that the barrier has harmed the audience and has helped their enemies; or he might appeal to the audience's sense of pity by arguing that the barrier has injured those with whom the audience identify themselves. In the *threat situation* the speaker might contend that the threat is strong enough to warrant their attention. Within this general *topoi,* the speaker might appeal to his audience's sense of fear, pity, anger, or emulation, by arguing respectively that the threat may harm the audience, has harmed friends of the audience, has destroyed valuable possessions, or has been overcome by people who faced similar threats. Finally, in the *identification situation* the speaker might argue that the audience should help another group. Within this general *topoi,* the speaker might appeal to his audience's sense of pity, friendship, and pride, by arguing that the particular group is in great need of help, that the group which needs help is made up of close friends of the audience, and that the audience can be proud of being the only ones in a position to help the group in distress.

An illustration of this method for employing *pathos* may be seen in a brief analysis of President John F. Kennedy's Inaugural Address.

After his introductory remarks, the President established a *goal-oriented* motivational situation and an *identification* motivational situation. He argued that the United States is determined to assure the survival and the success of liberty and that the United States will act for the benefit of all peoples of the world. Within the general *topoi,* President Kennedy appealed to his audience's sense of duty, confidence, determination, pride, friendship, strength, fear, justice, emulation, calmness, fairness, pity, and hope. He said:

> We dare not forget that we are the heirs of that first revolution. Let the word go forth from this time and place, to friends and foe alike, that the torch has been passed to a new generation of Americans — born in this century, tempered by war, disciplined by a hard and bitter peace, proud of our ancient heritage — and unwilling to witness or permit the slow undoing of those human rights to which this nation has always been committed, and to which we are committed today at home and around the world.
>
> Let every nation know, whether it wishes us well or ill, that we shall

pay any price, bear any burden, meet any hardship, support any friend, oppose any foe, in order to assure the survival and the success of liberty.

This much we pledge — and more.

To those old allies whose cultural and spiritual origins we share, we pledge the loyalty of faithful friends. United, there is little we cannot do in a host of cooperative ventures. Divided, there is little we can do — for we dare not meet a powerful challenge at odds and split asunder.

To those new states whom we welcome to the ranks of the free, we pledge our words that one form of colonial control shall not have passed away merely to be replaced by a far greater iron tyranny. We shall not always expect to find them supporting our view. But we shall always hope to find them strongly supporting their own freedom — and to remember that, in the past, those who foolishly sought power by riding the back of the tiger ended up inside.

To those peoples in the huts and villages of half the globe struggling to break the bonds of mass misery, we pledge our best efforts to help them help themselves, for whatever period is required — not because the communists may be doing it, not because we seek their votes, but because it is right. If a free society cannot help the many who are poor, it cannot save the few who are rich.

To our sister republics south of our border, we offer a special pledge — to convert our good words into good deeds — in a new alliance for progress — to assist free men and free governments in casting off the chains of poverty. But this peaceful revolution of hope cannot become the prey of hostile powers. Let all our neighbors know that we shall join with them to oppose aggression or subversion anywhere in the Americas. And let every other power know that this Hemisphere intends to remain the master of its own house.

To that world assembly of sovereign states, the United Nations, our last best hope in an age where the instruments of war have far outpaced the instruments of peace, we renew our pledge of support — to prevent it from becoming merely a forum for invective — to strengthen its shield of the new and the weak — and to enlarge the area in which its writ may run.[10]

The President next established a *threat* motivational situation, the threat being planned or accidental self destruction through the misuse of science. Within this general *topoi* President Kennedy appealed to his audience's sense of fear, friendship, and courage. He said:

Finally, to those nations who would make themselves our adversary, we offer not a pledge but a request: that both sides begin anew the quest for peace, before the dark powers of destruction unleashed by science engulf all humanity in planned or accidental self-destruction.

We dare not tempt them with weakness. For only when our arms are sufficient beyond doubt can we be certain beyond doubt that they will never be employed.

But neither can two great and powerful groups of nations take comfort from our present course — both sides overburdened by the cost of modern weapons, both rightly alarmed by the steady spread of the deadly atom, yet both racing to alter that uncertain balance of terror that stays the hand of mankind's final war.[11]

The President then established another *goal-oriented* motivational situation, encouraging the world's opponents to seek peace. Within this general *topoi* the President appealed to his audience's sense of calmness, courage, confidence, trust, friendship, hope, emulation, justice, and fair play. He said:

> So let us begin anew — remembering on both sides that civility is not a sign of weakness, and sincerity is always subject to proof. Let us never negotiate out of fear. But let us never fear to negotiate.
>
> Let both sides explore what problems unite us instead of laboring those problems which divide us.
>
> Let both sides, for the first time, formulate serious and precise proposals for the inspection and control of arms — and bring the absolute power to destroy other nations under the absolute control of all nations.
>
> Let both sides seek to invoke the wonders of science instead of its terrors. Together let us explore the stars, conquer the deserts, eradicate disease, tap the ocean depths, and encourage the arts and commerce.
>
> Let both sides unite to heed in all corners of the earth the command of Isaiah — to "undo the heavy burdens . . . [and] to let the oppressed go free."
>
> And if a beachhead of cooperation may push back the jungle of suspicion, let both sides join in creating a new endeavor, not a new balance of power, but a new world of law, where the strong are just and the weak secure and the peace preserved.[12]

President Kennedy next established a *difficulty* motivational situation and a *barrier* motivational situation. He contended that achieving world peace will be extremely difficult, and that the people of the world will have to tear down the barriers of tyranny, poverty, disease, and war. Within these general *topoi,* the President appealed to his audience's sense of courage, pride, duty, emulation, pity, determination, hope, and anger. He said:

> All this will not be finished in the first 100 days. Nor will it be finished in the first 1,000 days, nor in the life of this administration, nor even perhaps in our lifetime on this planet. But let us begin.
>
> In your hands, my fellow citizens, more than in mine, will rest the final success or failure of our course. Since this country was founded, each generation of Americans has been summoned to give testimony to its national loyalty. The graves of young Americans who answered the call to service surround the globe.
>
> Now the trumpet summons us again — not as a call to bear arms, though arms we need; — not as a call to battle, though embattled we are; — but a call to bear the burden of a long twilight struggle, year in and year out, "rejoicing in hope, patient in tribulation" — a struggle against the common enemies of man: tyranny, poverty, disease, and war itself.[13]

The President concluded his address by establishing another *goal-oriented* motivational situation, arguing that the people of the world should unite against the enemies of mankind. Within this general *topoi* the President appealed to his audience's sense of confidence, courage, pride, duty, friendship, justice, and love. He said:

> Can we forge against these enemies a grand and global alliance, north and south, east and west, that can assure a more fruitful life for all mankind? Will you join in that historic effort?
>
> In the long history of the world, only a few generations have been granted the role of defending freedom in its hour of maximum danger. I do not shrink from this responsibility — I welcome it. I do not believe that any of us would exchange places with any other people or any other generation. The energy, the faith, the devotion which we bring to this endeavor will light our country and all who serve it — and the glow from that fire can truly light the world.
>
> And so, my fellow Americans: ask not what your country can do for you — ask what you can do for your country.
>
> My fellow citizens of the world: ask not what America will do for you, but what together we can do for the freedom of man.
>
> Finally, whether you are citizens of America or citizens of the world, ask of us the same high standards of strength and sacrifice which we ask of you. With a good conscience our only sure reward, with history the final judge of our deeds, let us go forth to lead the land we love, asking His blessing and His help, but knowing that here on earth God's work must truly be our own.[14]

In summary, President Kennedy attempted to persuade his audience emotionally by establishing *goal-oriented, identification, difficulty, barrier,* and *threat* motivational situations; by selecting general *topoi* or lines of argument which coordinated with the general motivational situations; and by employing specific emotional appeals which coordinated with the general *topoi,* and which were designed to arouse in the hearers a sense of duty, confidence, determination, pride, friendship, strength, fear, justice, emulation, calmness, fairness, pity, hope, courage, trust, anger, and love.

Another example of the functional use of *pathos* is Pope Paul's address to the United Nations General Assembly, October 4, 1965. This address reveals *goal-oriented, difficulty, threat, barrier,* and *identification* motivational situations; general *topoi* that coordinate with the general motivational situations; and specific emotional appeals that coordinate with the general *topoi,* and that arouse the appropriate responses in the audience. (The text of this address appears in Appendix 3 of this book.)

By utilizing the techniques recommended and described in this section, preachers will be able to improve their communicative effectiveness. But again, concerned clergymen should read formal treatises on motivation to supplement this text and their understanding of the forces that impel human beings to act.

ETHOS

As stated earlier, *ethos* includes those materials that the speaker uses to establish himself as a person of intelligence, moral character, and goodwill, and the attempts of the speaker to use his *ethos* thus gained as a form of persuasive support.

A speaker may reveal his intelligence, for example, by displaying a sense of good taste, by acting with tact and moderation, and by using what is popularly called common sense. Probably the most impressive way to demonstrate one's intelligence is by showing a broad familiarity with historical and contemporary issues. For example, in his speech on "Today's Most Fateful Fact," delivered at McGill University, Montreal, Canada, on May 29, 1959, upon acceptance of the honorary degree Doctor of Laws, Adlai Ewing Stevenson displayed erudition with respect to historical and contemporary events by saying:

> In free nations, where no strict ideology is imposed from above, there are recurrent times of ferment and questioning. These are always times of turmoil and confusion. Old ideas are discarded, new directions sought, and sometimes in the midst of it all, it is not altogether easy to perceive the main areas of decision and the proper scope of the debate.
>
> Little more than a century ago, such a phase of questioning and revaluation was in full swing in Britain. The first onrush of the industrial revolution had changed the face of the land. It was a world of inhuman working hours, of child labor, of poverty herded into vast insanitary cities. And all this coexisted with great wealth and comfort for a few. "Two nations," wrote the wise Disraeli, of "privilege and the people," of "wealth and poverty," live side by side. Charles Dickens gave these "two nations" life and breath in his imperishable novels. Reformers — Lord Shaftesbury, the Christian Socialists, the free churches, the dogged forerunners of the labor movement — fought the widespread idea that no reform or intervention was possible since *laissez faire* had been preordained by an all-seeing Providence. And — ominously — Engels fed the evils of infant industrialism into the incendiary imagination of Karl Marx. Some decades afterwards a similar ferment was at work in America, sparking the reforming energies of William Jennings Bryan, Theodore Roosevelt, Woodrow Wilson and many other leaders of our post-Civil War period.
>
> What the reformers finally did was to create the conviction that no decent society could tolerate so wide a gulf between the "two nations."

In a hundred different methods of analysis and reform, they sought to establish reasonable methods of dealing with vast problems — and opportunities — unleashed by industrialism and by the wealth it created but did not equitably distribute among the creators.

I believe a comparable period of questioning and concern has opened in the West in the last decade. We face the end of the period of unquestioned Western supremacy. We face the rising claims of the vast majority of mankind. Some of the results of modernization have spread now to the whole human race, and once again the consequence of industrialism, undirected by broader aims of public policy, has been to recreate Disraeli's "two nations" in the world at large. One, a small minority of comparative wealth and privilege, lives in the main around the North Atlantic. Here in fortunate North America its per capita annual income is from $600 to $2,000. But the per capita income for two-thirds of humanity is not more than $100. In India, the greatest single democratic community in the world, the average is not much above $60 a head.

Here, then, repeated on a world scale in mid-20th century, are the riches and poverty side by side of mid-19th century England. And we would need the pen of a Dickens to paint the contrast between the comfortable dwellings of a thousand Western cities and the hovels of the miserable millions I have seen from Hong Kong to Johannesburg.[15]

A speaker may display intelligence by focusing attention on his objectivity. For example, at the close of the Constitutional Convention on September 17, 1787, Benjamin Franklin said:

I confess, that I do not entirely approve of this Constitution at present; but, Sir, I am not sure I shall never approve it; for, having lived long, I have experienced many instances of being obliged, by better information of fuller consideration, to change opinions even on important subjects, which I once thought right, but found to be otherwise. It is therefore that, the older I grow, the more apt I am to doubt my own judgment of others.[16]

A speaker may focus attention upon the probity of his character in several ways. First, he may associate himself with what his audience generally considers to be elevated and virtuous. For instance, when addressing the United Nations General Assembly on October 4, 1965, Pope Paul VI praised the United Nations for what they stood for and said that his message might be called "a moral and solemn ratification of this high Institution." [17] The Pope also stated that his voice symbolized the voices of those, for example, who condemn those who would try to renew wars, those who legitimately dream of a better human race, and those "who yearn for justice, for the dignity of life, for freedom, for well-being and progress." [18]

A second way to focus on the probity of one's character is to create the impression of being completely sincere in one's undertaking. For illustration, in his inaugural address, President John F. Kennedy stated:

We observe today not a victory of a party but a celebration of freedom — symbolizing an end as well as a beginning — signifying renewal, as well as change. For I have sworn before you and Almighty God the same solemn oath our forebears prescribed nearly a century and three quarters ago.

The world is very different now. For man holds in his mortal hands the power to abolish all forms of human poverty and all forms of human life. And yet the same revolutionary beliefs for which our forebears fought are still at issue around the globe — the belief that the rights of man come not from the generosity of the state but from the hand of God.

President Kennedy went on to underscore the nature of his commitment in the words quoted on pages 50 and 51, "Let the word go forth . . . that the torch has been passed to a new generation of Americans . . . tempered . . . disciplined . . . proud . . . we shall pay any price, bear any burden, meet any hardship, support any friend, oppose any foe to assure the survival and success of liberty." [19]

A third way to emphasize one's character is to rely upon authority derived from one's personal experience. Thus, in his address to a joint meeting of the United States Senate and House of Representatives on April 19, 1951, General Douglas MacArthur repeatedly relied upon authority derived from his fifty-two years of experience in military service.[20]

A fourth way to emphasize probity of character is to remove or minimize any unfavorable impressions of oneself or one's cause previously established by an opponent. For example, in his speech of April 19, 1951, General MacArthur said:

I have constantly called for the new political decisions essential to a solution. Efforts have been made to distort my position. It has been said, in effect, that I am a warmonger. Nothing could be further from the truth. I know war as few other men now living know it, and nothing to me is more revolting. I have long advocated its complete abolition as its very destructiveness on both friend and foes has rendered it useless as a means of settling international disputes.[21]

Finally, the fifth way a speaker may focus on the probity of his character is by associating the opposition or their cause with what is not virtuous. In 1833 John C. Calhoun argued against the Revenue Enforcement Bill by saying:

It has been said that the bill declares war against South Carolina. No. It decrees a massacre of her citizens! War has something ennobling about it, and, with all its horrors, brings into action the highest qualities, in-

> tellectual and moral. It was, perhaps, in the order of Providence that it should be permitted for that very purpose. But this bill declares no war, except, indeed, it be that which savages wage — a war, not against the community, but the citizens of whom that community is composed. But I regard it as worse than savage warfare — as an attempt to take away life under the color of law, without the trial by jury, or any other safeguard which the Constitution has thrown around the life of the citizen. It authorizes the President, or even his deputies, when they may suppose the law to be violated, without the intervention of a court or jury, to kill without mercy or discrimination![22]

A speaker may generate goodwill primarily through three methods. First, he may identify himself with his audience. Thus, in Pope Paul's address to the United Nations General Assembly, he said: "Thanks to all of you here present for your warm welcome. To each one of you We extend Our cordial and deferential greeting. Your friendship has invited Us and admits Us to this meeting; it is as a friend that We appear before you." [23]

A second major way to generate goodwill with one's hearers is to show a willingness to help them and those with whom the audience associates. An illustration of this is the speech, "I Have a Dream," which Dr. Martin Luther King, Jr., delivered on August 28, 1963.

Thirdly, a speaker displays goodwill by proceeding with candor and straightforwardness.

In general, the possibilities for the use of *ethos* are manifold, and any attempt to present an exhaustive classification of ethical appeals is futile. Clergymen should become more effective speakers if they utilize techniques which will magnify them as speakers of high moral character, well prepared on their subjects, and sincerely concerned about the welfare of their hearers. Preachers should adhere to Ralph Waldo Emerson's definition of eloquence — the art of speaking what you mean and are.

4
Structure

THE HISTORY OF PREACHING reveals certain periods in which sermons were delivered in church and then printed and widely disseminated to the populace. People sought to obtain copies of sermons in order to examine and discuss the focal ideas and meanings. Such periods of history are over, and today most sermons are presented and soon forgotten. However, there is the possibility that closer attention to structural components may prompt the public to examine and discuss contemporary sermons. If preachers were more concerned about the structure of their sermons, they probably would be more effective in influencing the convictions and actions of their hearers.

The purpose of this chapter is fivefold. First, it treats certain forms of behavior that occur in the listening situation and are relevant to structural consideration. Second, it presents a suggested outline format that is based upon the behavioral guidelines. Third, it offers suggestions for phrasing major concepts. Fourth, it offers a suggested sequence of steps for the construction of outlines. Finally, it briefly discusses extemporaneous versus manuscript forms of presentation as they relate to the outline.

LISTENING BEHAVIOR

Experiments reveal that the recall ability of most people in the listening situation is low. Some experts estimate that in most situations there is an immediate loss of 50 percent of the material orally presented. A knowledge of this phenomenon alone should prompt the clergy to construct outlines that aid the listener in recalling the message of the sermon.

Another form of behavior in the listening situation is that people tend to comprehend major ideas better than detailed information. Too many clergymen present conceptually complex sermons. They fail to understand that many people are unable to focus clearly on many concepts in a short period of time. Many theorists contend that people should talk more and more about less and less; that is, it is better to focus on only two or three concepts regardless of the length of the sermon.

A third form of behavior is that people tend to retain longer those concepts that are reinforced. The processes of repetition and restatement may be inculcated in the structure to assist retention capability. A deliberate placement of supporting material under each major concept should be mandatory in planning the outline. It seems that too many clergymen hope for divine inspiration to supply them with supporting material at the moment of utterance. This practice often results in metaphysical sermons meant for theological scholars rather than laymen in the congregation.

A fourth form of behavior is that people tend to comprehend short sentences better than long sentences. In planning the outline the speaker can phrase his major concepts and examine them for word count. While it is difficult to determine exactly what length makes a long concept, it is possible to eliminate words that are vague, general, or ambiguous. Only one aspect of a subject should be phrased in one major idea, thus avoiding multiple-oriented concepts and reducing the length of the concept. The appearance of conjunctives and punctuation often indicates that the idea is presented indirectly or that multiple ideas exist. By eliminating punctuation and conjunctives whenever possible, the preacher can shorten the sentence containing the major concept and thus establish clearer focus. An example of a long, complex, and indirectly phrased concept is: "Jesus, through his life and ministry shattered man-made barriers constructed by man's inhumanity to man, for example, the barriers of race and moral reputation." By applying the above suggestions, the preceding example may be stated: "Jesus shattered the race barrier through his ministry on earth."

A fifth form of behavior is that people tend to recall and comprehend summaries. While most summaries occur at the ends of sermons, if they occur at all, they may be employed usefully in the introductions as well. This is sometimes referred to as an initial summary. A minimum effort to present the main ideas in the introduction and to present them again in the conclusion should aid the hearers, because the speaker has given them a blueprint to follow in the introduction, and the listener has another opportunity to focus on the ideas in the conclusion.

A sixth form of behavior is that people tend to be influenced more by explicit messages than by implicit ones. The specific purpose or goal of a sermon should be stated explicitly so that the hearers do not draw their own inferences. If the message intended is implicit, then the preacher increases the possibility that his hearers will distort his intentions.

Observation reveals that some preachers fail to state their intentions explicitly, thus leaving their audience without a focal point for the sermon. Some speakers present a title as the essence of the specific purpose, but this generally is unsatisfactory because it is only a fragment of a complete thought. It is better to state explicitly that "A Christian should practice charity daily," than to state, "Today I want to talk about charity." Other clergymen present the explicit purpose at the end of the sermon. In this case, the audience has only a vague notion as to the focus of the message while they are listening; hence, the message is more implicit than explicit. The preacher is better advised to present his purpose in the introduction, lest he lose the attention of his audience because of the implicit nature of the message.

One of the most widely practiced techniques of sermon focus is to substitute a scriptural quotation for the specific goal of the sermon. Many of these quotations contain implicit messages that need focus and clarification for the hearer. Several examples may serve to clarify this distinction between the implicit nature of scriptural quotation and the explicit statement of the specific theme.

IMPLICIT:	EXPLICIT:
"For we are not ignorant of his designs" (2 Corinthians 2: 11).	Satan's stratagems are leveled at the destruction of Christianity.

"He [God] is not the God of the dead, but of the living" (Matthew 22:32).	There is a spiritual life after death.
"Do you not know that in a race all the runners compete, but only one receives the prize? So run that you may obtain it. Every athlete exercises self-control in all things. They do it to receive a perishable wreath, but we an imperishable. Well, I do not run aimlessly, I do not box as one beating the air; but I pommel my body and subdue it, lest after preaching to others I myself should be disqualified" (1 Corinthians 9:24-27).	Spiritual growth requires intensive effort.

Obviously the statements on the right are easier to retain.

A seventh form of behavior is that people tend to recall individual parts within the context of a pattern. To illustrate, consider the following numbers: 14142355641. If a pattern is applied to these digits, meaning is extracted and the parts more easily are recalled. A possible pattern is: 1 414 235-5641. Now the observer may recall a telephone pattern that indicates 1 as direct distance dialing, 414 as the area code, 235 as the local exchange, and 5641 as the specific number of a given party. When related to structure, this principle suggests that major ideas should be placed within a thought pattern. Some possible thought patterns are problem-solution; solution-problem; cause-effect; effect-cause; time sequence; spatial (i.e., east to west, top to bottom, inside to outside); antithetical (i.e., black and white, pro and con, good and bad); and classification (i.e., young and old, middle class, upper class, lower class).

The preacher may take any thought pattern and let it suggest the number and nature of the major ideas. For example, if he selects the problem-solution pattern, he would have two major ideas in the body of his sermon. The first main idea would state the essence of the problem, and the second main idea would state the essence of the solution. An example of this pattern may be employed in a sermon concerning the general topic of human selfishness. Two possible main ideas may be phrased: "We are plagued with the problem of human selfishness," and "The solution to this problem should begin in the home." In this case it is better to focus on two main concepts in a pattern sequenced for the entire sermon than to establish three subconcepts of the problem and five solutions all in one sermon. The main ideas are then amplified, clarified, and supported with material to establish them as the only two focal points of the sermon. Other aspects of the topic on human selfishness may be presented in another sermon at another time in order to effect reinforcement of a moral behavior over a longer period of time.

The following is a comparison between main ideas selected at random and main ideas established in a time sequence:

RANDOM ORDER:	*TIME SEQUENCE:*
1. Recounting and explanation of the gospel story in terms meaningful to modern man.	1. Standards of moral behavior were formed in the early days of Christianity.
2. The questions perplexing us today.	2. Standards of moral behavior today are being questioned by many.
3. The parable confronts us with the abiding fact and mystery of human sin.	3. Standards of moral behavior in the future will have to account for human sin.

It is probable that any audience would consider the topics on the right to be clearer than those on the left. Preachers must employ patterns if they wish to be influential in affecting the convictions and actions of their hearers.

THE GUIDELINES IN PERSPECTIVE

If the clergyman applies the preceding behavioral guidelines, the outline of a sermon assumes the following suggested topical format:

TITLE OF SERMON

I. Introduction
   A. Opening
   B. Specific Purpose
   C. Initial Presentation of Main Ideas

II. Discussion
   A. First Main Idea
      1. First Item of Support
   B. Second Main Idea
      1. First Item of Support

III. Ending
   A. Summary of Main Ideas
   B. Restatement of Specific Purpose
   C. Closing Remark

No rhetorical law or principle prescribes that the speaker must perform a certain action at a certain time in the order of a speech. The speaker may choose from a number of options which are based upon the best thinking and information presented by rhetorical theorists. The following outline is expanded to provide some possible options at each stage in the speech or sermon:

Title of Sermon (short, imaginative)

I. Introduction
   A. Opening Options
      1. Present the motivational rationale for speaking. Explain why the preacher should talk about the specific idea and why the congregation should listen to this idea at this particular time.
      2. Present an experience that relates to the specific purpose. It may be a personal experience of the preacher, or one that he observed or read about that was intense enough in its implications to motivate him to talk about it in the sermon. For example, a minister once opened a sermon by relating an informal discussion he had with a nine-year-old boy who was taking religious instructions in his church. The minister probed the boy's attitudes on racial discrimination and was so astounded by the feedback that this became the motivating factor for his sermon on Sunday.
      3. Present an item of support which is related to the subject matter. Possible forms of support are listed below in the discussion portion (Part II). For example, the preacher may open by defining a word that will be used often in the sermon in order to ad-

vance its meaning immediately and bring focus to the message he wishes to convey. Words such as "love," "peace," and "sin" are selected so often that clergymen proceed with the assumption that everyone holds the same meaning for the same word.

4. Scripture may be cited, but this is such a common device that many listeners may ignore it, especially if the message is implicit. Scripture may be the "silent" motivator, but it may be better to present it in the form of a specific purpose or as a form of support for a main idea.

B. Explicitly present the specific purpose of the sermon.

C. Clearly state each of the main points that will be discussed in Part II, and identify the thought pattern in relation to the main ideas

II. Discussion

A. Restate the first main idea.

1. Present the first item of support from the options listed below. Consider selecting items that have a real basis rather than a hypothetical construct. Much preaching is on an abstract plane, and it is through the selection of supporting material extracted from reality that the listener can discover how religious convictions or actions have meaning in a real society. For instance, it may be better to select a real example rather than a hypothetical one, or to make a comparison between two or more real people rather than hypothetical ones. The number of items of support selected for each main idea will depend on the amount of time for speaking.

a. An example
b. A definition
c. A statistic
d. A comparison
e. A quotation
f. A dialogue
g. An anecdote
h. An audio-visual aid
i. Any other forms of support that apply to the topic

B. Restate the second main idea.
   1. Present the first item of support.

III. Ending
   A. Summarize by restating the main ideas.
   B. Restate the specific purpose.
   C. Present the closing remark.

PHRASING THE SPECIFIC PURPOSE AND MAIN POINTS

To phrase the specific purpose and major points of a sermon, the preacher should adhere to the following procedures: First, establish one sentence for each concept. Second, construct a complete thought. Third, write each concept in a declarative sentence. Fourth, examine each word for clarity. Fifth, work toward phrasing each concept with as few words as possible. Sixth, establish only one focal point in each concept. Finally, determine whether the conceptual structure calls for a level of conviction, or action, or both.

SUGGESTED SEQUENCE IN OUTLINE CONSTRUCTION

To construct an outline for a sermon or other form of public speech, the minister should adhere to the following sequence: First, select and phrase the specific purpose. Second, select and phrase the main ideas. Third, select the specific thought pattern. Fourth, select the supporting material for each main idea. Fifth, select an opening motivational basis. Sixth, select a closing remark. Seventh, place all items on paper, using the numerical scheme suggested above.

EXTEMPORANEOUS AND MANUSCRIPT PRESENTATION

After preparing the outline, the clergyman either can convert the outline to a fully expanded manuscript, or can transfer the outline to note cards for an extemporaneous presentation. It is possible to use the fully expanded outline as speaking notes, but the tendency to read from it too much may lead to the speaker's forgetting to look directly at the audience. Conversion to a topical outline on note cards provides less of a barrier between the speaker and his audience.

5
Selection and Arrangement of Words

THE HISTORY OF PREACHING reveals that the English and American pulpits have endured patterns of two modal extremes. Preachers either have selected and arranged words plainly, or they have gone to stylistic excess for the sake of ostentatious display and impact. Indeed, it was a rare man who judiciously selected his language.

With the advent of the seventeenth century, the advent of science, and the awareness of the vernacular for popular discourse in both England and America, preachers followed the theory that plainness in preaching was the best course of action. Today, they have taken for granted a plain style of preaching.

THE ORAL MEDIUM

One major factor that preachers must consider if they intend to be effective in the pulpit is that written and oral skills are fundamentally different. An awareness and understanding of this factor may prompt a different attitude and practice that hopefully will strengthen the influence of sermons that are presented from the pulpit.

People often ask the question, "Do we write as we speak?" Can the minister compose a verbatim manuscript while he sits in his office or den and be homiletically brilliant? In all probability the answer is "No," for a speaker never writes to his audience in a face-to-face confrontation. One of the pitfalls of writing one's speech appears in Longinus' *On the Sublime*. Longinus noted that a preoccupation with figures of speech

> arouses a peculiar suspicion in the hearer's mind, a feeling of being deliberately trapped and misled. . . . He is easily angered by the thought that he is being outwitted like a silly child by the expert speaker's pretty figures; he sees in the fallacious reasoning a personal insult; sometimes he may altogether give way to savage exasperation, but even if he controls his anger he remains impervious to persuasion.[1]

Writing transcripts of sermons and homilies prompts the use of tools designed largely for poetic discourse. The concern of Longinus and other rhetorical theorists points out the pitfall of devotion to words and stylistic embellishment as an excess in writing. The preacher who does this today exercises the mechanics of discourse for print and not for a live audience. The judicious clergyman concentrates on the selection of ideas and thought rather than on individual words in the manuscript. The preparation leading to an extemporaneous delivery of sermons should make the preacher sensitive to the communication of concepts and should afford less time for consideration of the other elements of discourse.

Most rhetoricians will agree that consideration of style should follow conceptual analysis. The practice of writing words in an attempt to arrive at focal ideas in a manuscript prior to conceptual analysis supports the proposition that stylistically there is no difference between the oral and written media of communication. The avoidance of conceptual analysis also supposes that the mechanical manipulation of words generates preaching power.

Oral communication must be instantly intelligible. Herbert Spencer's law of economy dictates that one should speak or write in order that the listener or reader may comprehend quickly and accurately what is being communicated. It is imperative that this be done more in oral communication than in written discourse, for the reader can reread a given passage, whereas the listener cannot. Perhaps the writer who has done most to advance this concept is the late Professor William Norwood Brigance, who believed and taught that to write for the ear rather than the eye one must truly write aloud.

In written discourse the writer composes without the benefit of an audience in front of him and thus tends to think in terms of the universal conditions of God, man, and society. To be successful the preacher must depend upon his ability to concretize his discourse from the conception of an idea to the actual delivery of the concept. Professor Gladys Borchers of the University of Wisconsin discovered in her research about the distinctions between oral and written style that those who spoke adapted more to the audience and to the occasion by making repeated references to the people before them and the situation in which the speech occurred. Clergymen should not ignore the specific nature of their congregations and intone universals to live audiences. The oral medium demands and the listeners require of the clergy specific and immediate relevance.

In 1922, in *The Quarterly Journal of Speech Education,* Professor Charles H. Woolbert wrote one of the most analytical articles concerning the differences between speaking and writing. Woolbert contended, for example, that the speaker must concern himself with sounds, not marks on the printed page, and must concern himself with the enunciation and pronunciation of those sounds as fundamental tools of the oral medium. He contended that a printed word must have one meaning for the reader, whereas the spoken word may be tempered in meaning by the intonational and physical behavior of the speaker. And he contended that an audience has distracting stimulations, whereas the reader often is isolated in privacy and silence.[2] These are some of the unique characteristics of the oral medium which should influence homiletic practices.

The preacher who prepares for the oral medium must keep in mind the logical and psychological factors and variables. When in the pulpit, he would be wise to adapt to the oral medium, rather than to apply the tools designed mainly for the written medium. With this preliminary note on the nature of the oral medium, the preacher should be better equipped to approach the study of style and its application in the religious arena.

STYLE DEFINED

In 1783 Hugh Blair published his *Lectures on Rhetoric and Belles Lettres,* in which he defined style as "the peculiar manner in which a man expresses his conceptions, by means of language," and contended that "style has always some reference to an author's manner of thinking."[3] In 1851 Arthur Schopenhauer remarked in *The Art of Literature* that style is the "physiognomy of the mind" and "nothing but the mere silhouette of thought."[4]

And in 1888 in a lecture on the definitions of style the Rev. Austin Phelps stated that "style *is* thought. Qualities of style are qualities of thought."[5]

These definitions of style provide a useful point of departure, because they stress the relationship between the conceptual process and language. All of them endorse Quintilian's dictum that

> nothing should be done for the sake of words only, since words were invented merely to give expression to things: and those words are the most satisfactory which give the best expression to the thoughts of our mind and produce the effect which we desire upon the minds of the judges.[6]

This functional idea which Quintilian expressed is significant in that it postulates style as an indivisible element of the process of persuasion, and it focuses attention upon what language does rather than exclusively upon what language is. With this in mind, a final definition of style is now warranted.

Because the primary goal of the speaker is to secure a favorable response from the audience, and because the speaker's conceptual process and language pattern virtually are inseparable, style may be defined as the manner by which language is used to make ideas acceptable to a given audience.

STYLE ENHANCED

Joseph Addison is said to have once remarked that nothing in nature is so variable as a lady's hairdress. He should have added "unless it be the concept of stylistic quality," for probably no term has moved about more freely and has caused so much confusion as the term "stylistic quality." This is evidenced by the pervasive, fruitless, and even pernicious attempt by rhetoricians to compartmentalize the kinds of expression according to certain features or qualities.

Among the qualities of style found in rhetorical treatises are the grand, middle, plain, austere, periodic, loose, dry, elegant, florid, simple, labored, concise, diffuse, nervous, forceful, sonorous, rhapsodical, whimsical, precise, erudite, harsh, flowing, pure, hyperlatinistic, prosaic, firm, vivid, noble, sublime, perspicuous, weighty, dignified, penetrating, smooth, vehement, lucid, puerile, bold, energetic, stately, polished, apathetic, natural, brisk, frigid, patronizing, dogmatic, volatile, elaborated, involuted, opulent, terse, stoic, burlesque, libertine, and euphuistic.

The list is far from being exhaustive, and each quality has its own characteristics. To learn so many qualities is impractical and, perhaps, even impossible for the busy man of the cloth. Therefore, he should concentrate his time and energy in first learning only two stylistic qualities, namely clarity and impressiveness. The line of distinction between these qualities is not always clear; nor need it be, for the two qualities admittedly interact. However, clarity and impressiveness of style are the two most important stylistic instruments which, under appropriate and proper conditions, contribute to the effectiveness of the communicative act. Ideally, students of persuasion should learn other stylistic qualities, but only after they have mastered clarity and impressiveness of style.

OBSTACLES TO CLARITY

The following pages identify the most notorious obstacles to clarity, and illustrate the primary ways to make style impressive.

A. *Verbosity.* Arthur Schopenhauer wisely once remarked that a communicator should make sparing use of the hearer's time, patience, and attention, and that "to use many words to communicate few thoughts is everywhere the unmistakable sign of mediocrity. To gather much thought into few words stamps the man of genius." [7] All too often the pulpit violates this dictum. For example, common expressions are "because of the fact that" (instead of "because" or "since"); "in spite of the fact that" ("though" or "although"); "remind you of the fact that" ("remind you"); "the fact that he was present" ("his presence"); "It just happened the way it was bound to happen" ("It was inevitable"); and "We must choose between two courses of action, both of which have disadvantages" ("We face a dilemma").

Other forms of sermon doubletalk are "consensus of opinion," "present status quo," "first beginning," "round in shape," "large in size," "true facts," "each and every," "good advantages," "habitual customs," "mild and gentle," "peace and quiet" (with respect to physical noise), "rules and regulations," "null and void," "basic rudiments," "absolutely perfect," and "colorful rainbow." It should be easy to understand why people become confused while trying to interpret how, for example, "true facts" differ from "facts"; "round in shape" differs from "round"; "good advantages" differ from "advantages"; and "absolutely perfect" differs from "perfect." The clergy must remember that verbosity and clearness of thought often are incompatible.

B. *Profoundness.* Samuel Taylor Coleridge once said that "if men would only say what they have to say in plain terms, how much more eloquent they would be." [8] Consider the following examples that accentuate verbosity and profoundness.

A student once reported that "regardless of their pigmentation or coloration under normal illumination, felines of all species are cinereous when the earth becomes enveloped in tenebrosity." The student simply could have said that all cats are gray in the dark. A diplomat once "informed" his hearers that communism is permeated through and through "by the spirit of metaphysical monism, ethical and axiological relativism, self-centered, autonomous humanism, impersonalist collectivism, historical dynamism, and militant atheism." Indeed! But try to picture what the man stated.

The following words appeared in recent sermons by clergymen enrolled in a class on public speaking. Surely there are better words for a general audience.

unsubstantial	hypothesize	involuntariness
adventitious	conflagration	premonstration
consanguinity	corpulent	effectuation
deleterious	putrefaction	complacency
isagogic	egregious	peregrination
augmentation	elucidate	prevaricate
aporetic	transversion	emaciated
unveracious	desquamation	rusticate
adhortation	augurate	necessitous
concursus	proselytism	opprobrious
connatural	flusterate	manducation

C. *Over-conciseness.* Although verbosity may prove injurious to communication because it wastes time and clouds intelligibility, conciseness is not always virtuous. It is true that some of history's most powerful communications were brief. For example, Philip of Macedon is alleged to have threatened the Spartans by saying that, if he came to their land, he would exterminate them. The Spartans simply replied "If!" And what discourse on the vanity of human existence is more descriptive and concise than the words of Job?

> Man that is born of a woman
> is of few days, and full of trouble.

He comes forth like a flower, and withers;
he flees like a shadow, and continues not (Job 14:1-2).

However, precision of thought is impaired when the speaker fails to employ enough words. For example, a blunder resulting from overconciseness occurred when administrators in a western city put up a sign containing the following statute: "No vehicle drawn by more than one horse is allowed to cross this bridge in opposite directions at the same time." Also, the civil law of a western state once contained this statute: "All marriages of White persons and Negroes and Mulattoes are illegal and void." Because of being overly concise, the statute appears to assert that the only legally married persons in the state were Indians and Orientals. This is not what the administrators intended.

D. *Inaccurate syntax.* Syntactical integrity concerns the way in which a speaker assembles his words so as to convey his intended thoughts. The accurate assembling of words is a complex process best described in a standard textbook on grammar. Since the clergy have been taught for many years the basic and important aspects of language mechanics, this section is not a rehash of them. Instead, this section serves as a reminder that clearness of thought and the lack of syntactical integrity are incompatible, that the speaker must make certain that his word assemblage says what he wants it to say, and that he is deceiving himself if he believes he can use this complex process with only a meager knowledge of it.

The lack of syntactical integrity takes many forms, most of which are encountered in English classes. One type of syntactical error is the misplaced modifier. For instance, a minister concluded his eulogy on a former parishioner by saying, "Such was the end of our dear friend at the premature age of thirty-six." The speaker's construction does not make sense. How could the parishioner's age be premature? The minister should have said, "Such was the premature death of our friend at the age of thirty-six." The error was a misplaced modifier.

Dangling participles also violate syntactical integrity. Participles are verbal adjectives whose job is to modify some substantive in the sentence. The following examples help to illustrate the confusion that results when a speaker uses a participle but fails to provide a substantive for the participle to modify.

When a prominent scholar was to be inaugurated to the presidency of an eastern university, the minister appointed to deliver the inauguration address said, "Rev. Dr. . . . sir, having been elected president by the unanimous vote of the board of trustees and overseers of . . . University, I come on this behalf to induct you. . . ." The context asserts that the minister who delivered the address was the president-elect. This is not what the minister intended. In Tennessee a tombstone stated, "She lived a life of virtue, and died of cholera-morbus caused by eating green fruit in the hope of a blessed immortality. Go and do likewise." In England a tombstone stated: "Erected to the memory of . . ., shot accidentally, as a mark of affection by his brother." An express officer once remarked that his company was not responsible for "loss by fire, or the acts of God, or Indians, or other enemies of the Government." And a student newspaper once advertised, "For sale, German police dog; eats anything; very fond of children." These examples may be amusing, but they cloud communication.

Another violation of syntactical integrity occurs when sentence elements of unlike importance are linked together as equals. In other words, a less important element should be subordinate to a more important element. Consider the following sentence: "I stayed at home; I was ill." The speaker merely associated the two statements, whereas he should have shown the relation of one to the other. He might have said, "Because I was ill, I stayed at home." "Feeling ill, I stayed at home." Or, "I stayed at home, quite ill."

The speaker who identifies relationships, instead of leaving his audience to infer them, makes his hearers' task easier. Not only does such a speaker present facts, but also he integrates them. However, the speaker must be careful not to cause thoughtless and careless subordination. For instance, a careful speaker would say, "Because my head was feeling heavy, I took an aspirin." The thoughtless speaker would treat the motive for the act as if it were the matter of importance. The act itself would be relegated to the subordinate position. Preachers should bear in mind that careful consideration will make them appear as thoughtful speakers who carefully have selected their ideas and have arranged them with precision.

Weak parallelism also violates syntactical integrity. In its simplest terms parallelism means that like meanings should be put in like constructions. When a young minister was asked to describe his favorite sports, he replied. "I like hunting, fishing, golfing, and to bowl." The answer is confusing in that the minister mixed two noun forms of the verb, namely the gerunds "hunting," "fishing," and "golfing," and the infinitive "to bowl." He could have said, "I like hunting, fishing, golfing, and bowling." Or he could have said, "I like to hunt, fish, golf, and bowl." Listeners who are distracted by uncoordinated relations often fail to hear what immediately follows the structural errors, because they are too busy trying to extract the sense of what preceded the errors. The portion which the audience fails to grasp may well be the thesis or key idea of the address. When a speaker fails to convey his thesis, effective communication cannot occur.

A final violation of syntactical integrity is inaccurate pronoun reference. For example, an archbishop once remarked that "men look with an evil eye upon the good that is in others, and think that their reputation obscures them, and that their commendable qualities do stand in their light; and therefore they do what they can to cast a cloud over them." Who are "they"? Whom does "them" refer to? Who or what is "their"? What is the meaning of any of the pronouns in such a mess? Then there was the clergyman who reported that "the analytic approach in rhetorical criticism would be fine if one had a written copy of the speech or a tape recording and this is rarely found in the classroom situation." Does "this" refer to "a written copy of the speech" or to "a tape recording"?

Since syntactical integrity is so vital to clearness of thought, speakers should have a textbook on grammar in their working libraries and should use this textbook whenever doubt occurs as to the phrasing of a thought.

E. *Foreign language.* A wise man once remarked that just as a graft makes a gnarl in a tree, so does importation make a protuberance in a language. Because of their attachment to foreign languages, the clergy especially are guilty of using foreign terms freely in their discourses. Some foreignisms that appeared in recent sermons are: "terra firma," "tour de force," "una voce," "in aeternum," "in situ," "in toto," "lex terrae," "modus operandi," "per diem," and "ad infinitum."

The problem is that listeners often fail to comprehend the

meanings of the foreign phrases, and thus communication breaks down. When preparing future speeches, the clergy should ask, "What is the need for employing this foreign term or phrase when the vernacular is available?" If a speaker needs a foreignism to clarify his meaning, then he should use the foreignism. Words are made for thought, not thought for words. But if there is no need, then a speaker should not employ foreignisms.

F. *Equivocation.* Communication often breaks down because of equivocation, the assigning of two or more meanings for a particular word. To illustrate, a student made the statement: "The United World Federalists have many prominent members. For example, Washington, Adams, and Hamilton were Federalists. Hence, in the names of these great fathers of our country I appeal to you to support the United World Federalists." Notice that the word "Federalists" in the first sentence refers to a federation of various countries, whereas "Federalists" in the second sentence refers to a federation of American states. Speakers who equivocate usually confuse their hearers.

G. *Glittering and projectile adjectives.* Intelligibility frequently becomes hampered by adjectives which are highly emotional but also vague. For instance, what homogeneous image can an audience acquire from such words as "colossal," "lovely," "stupendous," "charming," "wonderful," "exquisite," "glorious," "awful," "elegant," "perfect," "fabulous," "tremendous," "terrible," "divine," "terrific," "ravishing," and "unbelievable"? Yet these words appear frequently in today's sermons.

Projectile adjectives also hinder communication. Projectile adjectives function not so much to present an objective description as to express the communicator's own feelings. Examples of projectile adjectives occurred when several students described a young man as "that poor, old guy"; a smiling person as "that miserable wretch"; a wealthy person as "that poor fellow"; and a tall, young woman as "the little old lady." Confusion occurs when the audience is uncertain whether the speaker's words are literal or figurative. Preachers must be careful in their descriptions.

H. *Nonfunctional imagery.* Imagery basically means the quality of words to evoke mental pictures. Clearness of thought demands clear imagery. A minister once referred to the "wilderness of mind" and to the "obscure climate of the human intellect."

What clear idea can one receive from the words "wilderness of mind"? What is an "obscure climate of the human intellect"? In fact, what is any climate of the mind? Such imagery blurs thought by taxing the hearer to discover resemblances which fail to exist. Imagery should be congruous with nature.

Mixed imagery also clouds intelligibility. A politician once stated that "Virginia has an iron chain of mountains running through her center, whch God placed there to milk the clouds and to be the source of her silver rivers." What corresponds to a chain of iron drawing milk from the clouds? Surely the imagery is vague.

Finally, communication should not be hindered by the use of learned and excessive imagery. All too often clergymen conceal their thoughts by employing imagery that only people familiar with the classics can interpret. The preceding examples fail to exhaust all of the obstacles to clearness of thought, but they sufficiently warn the clergy to be clear if persuasion is their objective.

IMPRESSIVENESS

As noted earlier, style is the manner by which language is used to make ideas acceptable to an audience. Clarity is one of the basic qualities of style, because it is essential to understanding. Impressiveness is the other basic quality, for it helps to fix ideas firmly in the minds of the hearers. To impress literally means to implant firmly on the mind or to fix in the memory. Impressiveness of style means those elements of language which intensify the effect upon either the mind or the feelings. The major ways of achieving impressiveness of style are imagery, figures of speech, and freshness in expression.

A. *Imagery.* Imagery is the ability of words to evoke mental pictures, and this ability is strengthened when the pictures involve real and intense sensory perceptions. Consider the following examples which appeal to the audience's sense of sight, hearing, smelling, touch, and motor-muscular reactions:

On December 27, 1859, Edwin Hubbell Chapin spoke on "Modern Chivalry," and urged his hearers:

> Think of men lighting their cigars in the trenches of the Redan, of the sergeant at the battle of the Alma, mortally wounded, and urged to give up the standard, still carrying it to the end of the action! Think of the

> helmsman on Lake Erie, who stood at the rudder of the burning vessel, while his hand cracked with the heat. . . . Think of the boy on the sinking steamer, touching off the sentinel gun! Think of the soldiers standing by their guns as the ship went down, and firing a *feu de joie* as the waves closed over them.[9]

On July 4, 1852, while discussing slavery, Frederick Douglass stated that if he could reach the nation's ear he would "pour out a stream of biting ridicule, blasting reproach, withering sarcasm, and stern rebuke. For it is not light that is needed, but fire; it is not the gentle shower, but thunder. We need the storm, the whirlwind, and the earthquake!"[10] And in 1877, while speaking on "The Sandwich Islands," Samuel Langhorne Clemens wrote:

> These Kanakas have some cruel instincts. They will put a live chicken in the fire just to see it hop about. In the olden times they used to be cruel to themselves. They used to tear their hair and burn their flesh, shave their heads, and knock out an eye or a couple of front teeth, when a great person or a king died — just to testify to their sorrow; and if their grief was so sore that they couldn't possibly bear it, they would go out and scalp a neighbor or burn his house down. And they used to bury some of their children alive when their families were too large.[11]

A speaker also might employ imagery by overtly identifying the specific senses to which he appeals. For instance, one of the great preachers in colonial America, Samuel Davies, said in his sermon on "The General Resurrection":

> Once indeed I received sensations of pleasure from thee, but now thou art transformed into an engine of torture. No more shall I through thine eyes behold the cheerful light of the day, and the beautiful prospects of nature, but the thick glooms of hell, grim and ghastly ghosts, heaven at an impassable distance, and all the horrid sights of woe in the infernal regions. No more shall thine ears charm me with the harmony of sounds, but terrify and distress me with the echo of eternal groans, and the thunder of almighty vengeance! No more shall the gratification of thine appetites afford me pleasure, but thine appetites, forever hungry, forever unsatisfied, shall eternally torment me with their eager importunate cravings. No more shall thy tongue be employed in mirth, and jest, and song, but complain, and groan, and blaspheme, and roar forever. Thy feet, that once walked in the flowery enchanted paths of sin, must now walk on the dismal burning soil of hell.[12]

The preceding examples reveal that the principle of imagery lies in the heightened perception that results when sensory experiences are created or recreated in memory, through the use of words. Clergymen would be wise to employ functional imagery in their sermons and other public speeches.

B. *Figures of speech.* By themselves figures of speech may

have decorative value, but such decoration is insignificant if the figures fail to reinforce the speaker's main thoughts. In other words, figures of speech must be functional. Their primary task is to reinforce thought; they must never stand as substitutes for reason. The following figures of speech add both clarity and impressiveness to style when used appropriately:

1. *Allegory* is an extended metaphor in which objects and persons in a narrative are equated with meanings that lie outside the narrative itself. The characters usually are personifications of abstract qualities, and the action and setting represent the relationship among the abstractions. The speaker should present these materials in a manner that represents meanings independent of the action described in the surface story. The meanings may be religious, moral, political, or social.

Famous examples of allegory are Spenser's *The Faerie Queene,* Bunyan's *Pilgrim's Progress,* and Swift's *Gulliver's Travels.* Consider also the allegory that appears in John Leland's sermon on "The Jarrings of Heaven Reconciled by the Blood of the Cross," delivered in Grafton, Massachusetts, in the early nineteenth century. Leland said:

> at the instance of Justice, Omnipotence arose like a lion from the swellings of Jordan; made bare His thundering arm, high raised His brandished sword, waved His iron rod, and advanced toward the rebel with hasty strides.
>
> *Love* cried, Forbear, I can not endure the sight!
>
> The *Law* replied, Cursed is everyone that continueth not in all things written in the law to do them. The soul that sins, shall die.
>
> *Grace* exclaimed, Where sin hath abounded, grace shall much more abound!
>
> *Truth* said, In the day that thou transgressest thou shalt surely die!
>
> *Mercy* proclaimed, Mercy rejoiceth against judgment!
>
> *Justice,* with piercing eye, and flaming tongue, said, "Strike! strike! strike the rebel dead! and remove the reproach from the throne of heaven.[13]

2. *Alliteration* is the repetition of the same consonant sound at the beginning of two or more words immediately succeeding each other, or at short intervals. Some examples of rhythm through alliteration are: "suffered the severest setback," "masses of mankind," "prone to prosper and protect," "mass misery," "form of force," "sacrificed to security," "vitality and vigilance," "community and communion," "battle between brotherhood," "positive power and protection," and "dark and daring."

3. *Anastrophe* is the deliberate inversion of the usual, normal, or logical order of the parts of a sentence. Like alliteration, anastrophe secures rhythm and gains emphasis. For illustration, in his funeral oration for Louis Bourbon, delivered in the Cathedral of Notre Dame in the seventeenth century, James Bossuet asked: "That gifts like these come from God, who can doubt? That they are worthy of admiration, who does not see?"[14] In his sermon on "The First Five Minutes After Death" Henry Parry Liddon said, "Like death itself, the solemnities which follow it must come to all of us. We know not when, or where, or how we shall enter in; this only we know — that it must."[15]

4. *Andiplosis* generates emphasis by repeating the last word or words of one sentence at the beginning of the following sentence. Andiplosis was used on July 25, 1848, when Joseph Mazzini said before a mass meeting in Milan: "And love, young men, love and venerate the ideal. The ideal is the Word of God."[16] On December 5, 1963, Hon. Don Fuqua of Florida stated: "I watched for a long while from the hillside, as a steady stream of Americans trudged up the embankment. It was quiet, it was reverent, it was sad — but in a sense, it was proud. Proud of the man whose memory this silent march commemorated."[17] Also on December 5, 1963, Hon. Leonor Kretzer Sullivan of Missouri stated that "prior to his administration, we were often told, we who serve in elective office, that politics had no appeal to youth. Youth, we were told, looked upon political activity as self-serving and somehow not quite respectable."[18]

5. *Antimachus* defines a thing in terms of what it is not. Edmund Burke used this figure on March 22, 1775, when making a last desperate plea for conciliation with the American colonies, stating:

> The proposition is peace. Not peace through the medium of war; not peace to be hunted through the labyrinth of intricate and endless negotiations; not peace to arise out of universal discord, foemented *[sic]* from principle, in all parts of the empire; not peace to depend on the juridical determination of perplexing questions, or the precise marking the shadowy boundaries of a complex government. It is simple peace sought in the spirit of peace, and laid in principles purely pacific.[19]

6. *Antimetabole* is the repetition of certain words in successive clauses or sentences, but in reversed order. For example, when objecting to taxation without representation on January 14, 1766,

William Pitt told the House of Commons, "You have prohibited where you ought to have encouraged. You have encouraged where you ought to have prohibited."[20] On December 5, 1963, Hon. John W. McCormack of Massachusetts said that John F. Kennedy "was a President who had taken hold of his education and whose education had taken hold of him to the immense benefit of his countrymen and to the enhancement of the prestige of the White House for all time."[21] In his inaugural address John F. Kennedy said, "Let us never negotiate out of fear. But let us never fear to negotiate."[22] He also stated, "And so, my fellow Americans: Ask not what your country can do for you—ask what you can do for your country."[23]

7. *Antithesis of idea* contrasts clauses and sentences. For instance, in January 1831, Thomas Babington Macaulay argued that the possibility that

> a Jew should be a judge in a Christian country would be most shocking. But he may be a juryman. He may try issues of fact; and no harm is done. But if he should be suffered to try issues of law, there is an end of the Constitution. He may sit in a box plainly dressed, and return verdicts. But that he should sit on the bench in a black gown and white wig, and grant new trials, would be an abomination not to be thought of among baptized people.[24]

Macaulay also contended:

> It would be impious to let a Jew sit in Parliament. But a Jew may make money; and money may make members of Parliament. Gatton and Old Sarum may be the property of a Hebrew. An elector of Penryn will take ten pounds from Shylock rather than nine pounds nineteen shillings and elevenpence three farthings from Antonio. To this no objection is made. That a Jew should possess the substance of legislative power, that he should command eight votes on every division as if he were the great Duke of Newcastle himself, is exactly as it should be. But that he should pass the bar and sit down on those mysterious cushions of green leather, that he should cry "hear" and "order," and talk about being on his legs, and being, for one, free to say this and to say that, would be a profanation sufficient to bring ruin on the country.[25]

8. *Antithesis of word* contrasts specific words. For an illustration, on August 2, 1826, Daniel Webster said, "Sink or swim, live or die, survive or perish, I give my hand and my heart to this vote."[26] On December 5, 1963, Hon. Carl Albert of Oklahoma stated:

> John Kennedy was a man of tough mind and tender heart, of great passion and iron self-discipline. A man for work and a man for play. A man for joy and a man for suffering. A man for the heads of state and a man

for little children. A man for the old and ill, a man for the youthful and strong.[27]

9. *Apophasis* enables a speaker to make an assertion while seeming to suppress or deny it. For example, in his sermon on "The Greatness of St. Paul," John Chrysostom said, "I love Rome even for this, although indeed one has other grounds for praising it, both for its greatness, and its antiquity, and its beauty, and its populousness, and for its power, and its wealth, and its successes in war. But I let all this pass. . . ."[28] In his sermon on "Is There Nothing Steadfast in Our World?" Douglas Horton stated that "no one can go up and down the land in these days without being made aware that our people are in a state — I shall not say of hysteria, though the word is not too strong to describe the conditions of some — but at least of anxiety."[29]

10. *Apostrophe* displays deep emotional expression by directly addressing some abstract quality, or nonexistent personage, or someone not present in the immediate audience. For example, while speaking on American independence, Samuel Adams exclaimed:

> Immortal spirits of Hampden, Locke, and Sidney! will it not add to your benevolent joys to behold your posterity rising to the dignity of men, and evincing to the world the reality and expediency of your systems, and in the actual enjoyments of that equal liberty, which you were happy, when on earth in delineating and recommending to mankind![30]

When eulogizing Henri De La Tour-D'Auvergne on January 10, 1676, Esprit Flechier exclaimed, "O death, too sudden!"[31] While speaking in the Senate of the United States, November 25, 1963, the Rev. Frederick Brown Harris said, "God of the living and of the living dead: as in this hour we bow in the shadow of a people's grief, Thou dost hear the sobbing of a stricken nation."[32]

11. *Asyndeton* expresses vehemence and speed by being a form of condensed expression in which words or short phrases, usually joined by conjunctions, are presented in series, separated only by commas. The following quotations illustrate this figure of speech: When speaking about St. Stephen, Martin Luther said:

> Who can number the virtues illustrated in Stephen's example? There loom up all the fruits of the Spirit. We find love, faith, patience, benevolence, peace, meekness, wisdom, truth, simplicity, strength, consolation, philanthropy.[33]

On June 3, 1879, Robert G. Ingersoll eulogized his brother by saying, "the loved and loving brother, husband, father, friend died, where manhood's morning almost touches noon, and while the shadows still were falling toward the West." [34] On December 5, 1963, Hon. Joseph P. Addabbo of New York said that "History and the future can only prove the real greatness of John Fitzgerald Kennedy—President, father, husband, son, brother, war hero." [35]

12. *Climax* generates balance and emphasis by passing to a word only after advancing by steps through the prerequisite words. For instance, in his sermon on "The Two Tentmakers," Reverend Russell Cartwright Stroup alluded to the idle rich who gather at the Riviera to be amused, and stated that "when they are bored with gambling they eat and when they are bored with eating they dance, and when they are bored with dancing they make love and when they are too bored for anything they get drunk and are put to bed." [36] On August 17, 1962, John F. Kennedy stated that "Water is our most precious asset—and its potential uses are so many and so vital that they are sometimes in conflict: Power versus irrigation, irrigation versus navigation, navigation versus industrial, industrial versus recreational." [37]

13. *Elimination* enumerates several possibilities but one. As an illustration, on March 28, 1775, Patrick Henry stated before the Virginia Convention of Delegates:

> And what have we to oppose to them? Shall we try argument? Sir, we have been trying that for the last ten years. Have we anything new to offer on the subject? Nothing. We have held the subject up in every light of which it is capable; but it has been all in vain. Shall we resort to entreaty and humble supplication? What terms shall we find which have not been already exhausted? Let us not, I beseech you, sir, deceive ourselves longer. Sir, we have done everything that could be done, to avert the storm which is now coming on. We have petitioned; we have remonstrated; we have supplicated; we have prostrated ourselves before the throne, and have implored its interposition to arrest the tyrannical hands of the ministry and Parliament. Our petitions have been slighted; our remonstrances have produced additional violence and insult; our supplications have been disregarded; and we have been spurned, with contempt, from the foot of the throne. In vain, after these things, may we indulge the fond hope of peace and reconciliation. There is no longer any room for hope. If we wish to be free—if we mean to preserve inviolate those inestimable privileges for which we have been so long contending—if we mean not basely to abandon the noble struggle in which we have been so long engaged, and which we have pledged ourselves never to abandon until the glorious object of our contest shall be obtained, we must fight! I repeat it, sir, we must fight! An appeal to arms and to the God of Hosts is all that is left us! [38]

14. *Ellipsis* is the omission of one or more words which, while essential to the grammatical structure of the sentence, can be easily supplied by the hearer. This figure of speech may generate emphasis if the words to be supplied occur in proper grammatical form not too remote from the place where the ellipsis occurs. For example, in his sermon on "Do You Believe in Love" Bishop Herbert Welch asked: "How could you teach any man courage if there were no fears to fight, no threats to overcome? How [could you] teach him kindness if there was no suffering to be relieved?" [39] In his sermon on "The Fifth Anniversary of the Victory of Monte Cassino," Bishop Joseph F. Gawlina said that "the apex (archimedal point) of our future, therefore, is religion; our sabre and shield, the Gospel." [40]

15. *Epanaphora* is characterized by sentences or several members of sentences beginning with the same word or phrase. As an illustration, on February 19, 1788, Edmund Burke said in the opening speech at the trial of Warren Hastings:

> I impeach Warren Hastings, Esquire, of high crimes and misdemeanors.
>
> I impeach him in the name of the Commons of Great Britain, in Parliament assembled, whose parliamentary trust he has betrayed.
>
> I impeach him in the name of all the Commons of Great Britain, whose national character he has dishonored.
>
> I impeach him in the name of the people of India, whose laws, rights, and liberties he has subverted, whose property he has destroyed, whose country he has laid waste and desolate.
>
> I impeach him in the name, and by virtue, of those eternal laws of justice which he has violated.
>
> I impeach him in the name of human nature itself, which he has cruelly outraged, injured, and oppressed, in both sexes, in every age, rank, situation, and condition of life.[41]

On December 11, 1963, Hon. Stephen M. Young of Ohio stated that "there has been too much hate built up by unscrupulous demagogs—hate for President Kennedy, hate for his administration; hate for the Chief Justice of the United States; hate unbridled." [42]

16. *Epistrophe* is the conclusion of sentences or clauses with the same word or phrase. For instance, on April 19, 1780, Henry Grattan said in the Irish House of Commons that "a country enlightened as Ireland, armed as Ireland, and injured as Ireland, will be satisfied with nothing less than liberty." [43] On June 10, 1963, John F. Kennedy said that "the United States, as the world

knows, will never start a war. We do not want a war. We do not now expect a war."[44] In his sermon on "The Best Things in the Worst Times," the Rev. James A. Pike said that "Julius Caesar wanted one world; Adolf Hitler wanted one world; today the Communists want one world."[45]

17. *Epizeuxis* is the repetition of a word without intervening words. This figure of speech differs from andiplosis in that the latter deals with two sentences, whereas epizeuxis occurs within one sentence. For example, on November 18, 1777, Lord Chatham stated, "If I were an American, as I am an Englishman, while a foreign troop was landed in my country, I never would lay down my arms —never—never—never."[46] On October 4, 1965, Pope Paul VI said, "Never again war, war never again!"[47]

18. *Gradualism* generates emphasis by moving from a lesser to a greater degree of quality or quantity. For example, in his inaugural address President John F. Kennedy stated that "this will not be finished in the first 100 days. Nor will it be finished in the first 1,000 days, nor in the life of this administration, nor even perhaps in our lifetime on this planet."[48] Also on December 5, 1963, Hon. Page Belcher of Oklahoma stated that President Kennedy's "dedication to public service gave to this country a Navy lieutenant, a Congressman, a Senator, and a President."[49]

19. *Homoeoteleuton* is the repetition of similar word endings. For example, on February 5, 1957, Rabbi Charles E. Shulman stated that "there are four philosophies in our time followed by men. One of them is cynicism. One is nihilism. One is materialism. And one is idealism."[50] On December 5, 1963, Hon. Torbert H. Macdonald of Massachusetts stated that he had seen President Kennedy "grow and mature physically, mentally, and morally."[51]

20. *Hyperbole* is conscious exaggeration without the intent of literal persuasion. While debating Stephen Douglas at Quincy, Illinois, October 13, 1858, Abraham Lincoln asked, "Is not that running his Popular Sovereignty down awfully? Has it not got down as thin as the homoeopathic soup that was made by boiling the shadow of a pigeon that had starved to death?"[52] On December 22, 1876, Samuel Langhorne Clemens spoke on New England weather and stated:

> In the spring I have counted one hundred and thirty-six different kinds of weather inside of four and twenty hours. It was I that made the fame

and fortune of that man that had that marvelous collection of weather on exhibition at the Centennial that so astounded the foreigners. He was going to travel all over the world and get specimens from all the climes. I said: "Don't you do it; you come to New England on a favorable spring day." I told him what we could do, in the way of style, variety, and quantity. Well, he came, and he made his collection in four days. As to variety – why, he confessed that he got hundreds of kinds of weather that he had never heard of before. And as to quantity – well, after he had picked out and discarded all that was blemished in any way, he not only had weather enough, but weather to spare; weather to hire out; weather to sell; to deposit; weather to invest; weather to give to the poor.[53]

21. *Hypophora* is the asking of a question followed by the immediate answer to the question. For example, while arguing over a system of protection of American industry, March 30-31, 1824, Henry Clay said that

> the South cannot exert its industry and enterprise in the business of manufactures! Why not? The difficulties, if not exaggerated, are artificial, and may, therefore, be surmounted. But can the other sections embark in the planting occupations of the south? The obstructions which forbid them are natural, created by the immutable laws of God, and, therefore, unconquerable.[54]

When eulogizing President Kennedy on December 11, 1963, Hon. Karl E. Mundt of South Dakota said, "What is the one characteristic of this man that stands most firm in my mind? I would term it his phenomenal capacity for growth."[55]

22. *Indecision* is the feigned uncertainty of how to say what follows. In his sermon on "Obedience the True Test of Love to Christ," delivered September 16, 1781, Robert Robinson said that "there are in His disciples such things as render their love to Christ – what shall I say – suspicious? suspicious? Is that the word?"[56] In his sermon on "Future Punishment" Henry Ward Beecher said that "Theodore Parker himself declared, I think – I may be mistaken; but if I recollect right he declared – that the first three gospels left no doubt in his mind that Christ did preach the doctrine of future and eternal punishment."[57]

23. *Interplacement* is the repetition of the first and last words of successive clauses or sentences. For example, on October 7, 1831, while arguing in the House of Lords for the acceptance of the Reform Bill, Henry Brougham said, "By all you hold most dear – by all the ties that bind every one of us to our common order and our common country, I solemnly adjure you – I warn you – I implore you – yea, on *my bended knees,* I sup-

plicate you—reject not this bill!"[58] On November 22, 1963, John F. Kennedy declared: "Without the United States, South Vietnam would collapse overnight. Without the United States, the SEATO alliance would collapse overnight. Without the United States, the CENTO alliance would collapse overnight."[59] On December 5, 1963, Hon. Robert N. Giaimo of Connecticut said:

> If we must search for blame—and it is inherent in us that we must—let us all share it. Let each of us who has ever known a complacent moment bear the blame. Let each of us who ignored the fury of hate and extremism bear the blame. And let each of us who thought more of self than the rights and future of others bear the blame.[60]

24. *Irony* is the use of a word in such a way as to convey a meaning opposite the literal meaning of the word. A good illustration of this is found in the classic funeral oration in which Antony frequently called Brutus an "honorable man." Irony often is confused with sarcasm, but it differs in that it usually is lighter than sarcasm—that is, it is less harsh in its wording though in effect probably more cutting because of its indirectness.

25. *Isocolon* is characterized by sentence elements being similar not only in structure but also in length, i.e., the number of words or even syllables. For instance, in his sermon on "The Joyful Sound of Salvation" Cotton Mather alluded to "the grace that will pardon the penitent! The grace that will quicken the impotent!"[61] In his sermon on "Spared!" Charles Haddon Spurgeon said, "If I am left, why am I left? Why am I not taken home to heaven? Why do I not enter into my rest?"[62] In his remarks as prepared for delivery on November 22, 1963, John F. Kennedy stated that "this Nation's strength and security are not easily or cheaply obtained—nor are they quickly and simply explained."[63] He also said, "Dollar for dollar, in or out of government, there is no better form of investment in our national security than our much-abused foreign aid program. We cannot afford to lose it. We can afford to maintain it."[64]

26. *Litotes* is a form of understatement in which a thing is affirmed by stating the negative of its opposite. For example, common expressions are "She's not half bad," "He's no spring chicken," "She was not unsympathetic," and "She's no raving beauty."

27. *Metaphor* is an implied comparison which identifies one subject with another and ascribes to the first, one or more of the qualities of the second. For example, on December 11, 1963, Hon. A. S. Mike Monroney of Oklahoma stated that "in advocating and promoting legislation he [John F. Kennedy] seldom launched a play for short yardage. He went for a touchdown every time." [65] On December 5, 1963, Hon. James C. Wright, Jr., of Texas stated:

> Mr. Speaker, when the petals of a rose are crushed, a fragrance lingers in the atmosphere.
>
> The life of John Fitzgerald Kennedy inspired and beautified our world. It was the finest and most perfectly formed rose in our garden. Now, so unspeakably crushed in the full flower of its beauty, its fragrance is all about us.[66]

28. *Metonymy* is the substitution of a term naming an object closely associated with the word in mind for the word itself. On July 19, 1848, at the First Woman's Rights Convention, Seneca Falls, Elizabeth Cady Stanton used metonymy when she said that the women of America would strive to enlist "the pulpit and the press in their behalf." [67] Examples of metonymy which recently appeared in sermons are "a victim of the bottle" (alcoholic), "the Bench" (Judge), "the Bar" (Lawyers), "the Chair" (Chairman), "the Brass" (commissioned officers), "the White House" (the President), "the pulpit" (the clergy), "the hammer and sickle" (communism), "the ballot" (voting), and "a strange tongue" (language).

29. *Onomatopoeia* is the use of words which in their pronunciation suggest their meaning. For example, in his sermon on "The Great Assize" the Reverend John Wesley alluded to "Aetna, Heela, Vesuvius, and all the other volcanoes that belch out flames and coals of fire." [68] Other examples of onomatopoeia are "hiss," "slam," "buzz," "whirr," "sizzle," and "shriek."

30. *Oxymoron* generates sharp emphasis by bringing together two contradictory terms. For instance, when speaking on "Christ's Triumph in the Resurrection," John Donne said, "That particular, that general particular (if we may say so, for it includes all) which all were to know. . . ." [69] While speaking at the eleventh annual dinner of the New England Society of St. Louis, December 21, 1895, Henry C. Caldwell told the story about a Kentuckian who wanted to be released from jail so that

he could return to Kentucky and "fight in peace." [70] Other examples are "turn its smoothness rough," "silently voiced," "the silence is deafening," "a sad optimist," "a cheerful pessimist," "sweet-sour pickle," "a wise fool," "an honest thief," "harmonious discord," "a huge midget," "a loud whisper," and "love is a healthy sickness."

31. *Parallelism* is an arrangement of parts of a sentence and larger units of composition by which one element of equal importance with another is equally developed and similarly phrased. For illustration, on November 19, 1863, Abraham Lincoln stated that "in a larger sense, we cannot dedicate — we cannot consecrate — we cannot hallow — this ground," and "that government of the people, by the people, for the people shall not perish from this earth." [71] And in his inaugural address President John F. Kennedy stated, "Let every nation know, whether it wishes us well or ill, that we shall pay any price, bear any burden, meet any hardship, support any friend, oppose any foe to assure the survival and success of liberty." [72]

32. *Parenthesis* is the insertion of some verbal unit in a position that interrupts the normal syntactical flow of a sentence. For example, on August 31, 1837, when speaking on the American scholar, Ralph Waldo Emerson stated that "it is a sign — is it not? — of new vigor, when the extremities are made active, when currents of warm life run into the hands and the feet." [73] On December 11, 1963, Hon. Frank Church of Idaho said that "I am inclined to believe — though tomorrow could easily prove me wrong — that of the work he [J. F. Kennedy] finished, during his brief tenure, the nuclear weapons test ban treaty will stand out above all other accomplishments." [74] On December 5, 1963, Hon. Florence P. Dwyer of New Jersey said that President Kennedy "was no visionary. His dreams — if, indeed, they could be called dreams — were made of solid stuff, the product of an active intellect, tempered by an acute awareness of what at any one time was practical." [75]

33. *Paronomasia* involves a play on words. For instance, on December 22, 1880, Horace Porter informed his hearers that "the poor Chinese have been driven away. They have been driven away from many places by that formidable weapon — the only weapon which Dennis Kearney has ever been able to use against them — the Chinese must-get." [76] On January 29, 1895, Tunis

Garret Bergen said that when Manhattan Island was purchased from the Indians, "It abounded in swamps, and the few streams that meandered through the rocks were so shallow and sluggish that even the beavers thought they were not worth a damn." [77] On December 7, 1891, while lecturing on "American Wit and Humor," Minot Judson Savage stated:

> Why is there no need of people's being hungry in the desert? Because of the sand which is there. How did the sandwiches come there? Ham and his descendants were bred and mustered there. Yes, but besides ham and bread and mustard, a perfect sandwich needs some butter: how did they get the butter? Why, when Lot was driven out of Sodom, his wife was turned into salt, and all the family butter ran into the desert.[78]

34. *Personification* endows animals and concrete inanimate objects with human form, character, or sensibilities. For illustration, while lecturing on the work of universities in the South, Benjamin Harvey Hill stated that:

> Our tired soil will strike up a song like unto Miriam's, when it feels the touch of accomplished skill. Our ores will leap from their beds, and in ringing mirth make and feel active machinery. . . . Our waterfalls, wearied from the solos of centuries, will join in musical duets with the shuttle and loom.[79]

35. *Polysyndeton* abounds in conjunctive particles to heighten or magnify one's ideas. For example, on April 6, 1933, while speaking on owning books, William Lyon Phelps stated that "in a private library, you can at any moment converse with Socrates or Shakespeare or Carlyle or Dumas or Dickens or Shaw or Barrie or Galsworthy." [80] On December 5, 1963, Hon. William H. Bates of Massachusetts called the assassination of President Kennedy a tragedy, and stated that "an emperor, a chancellor, presidents, queens, prince of state and church, a mourning world was the cast. No one, not Aeschylus, nor Sophocles, nor Euripides, nor Shakespeare, nor Dumas, nor Beaumarchais had ever attempted to rival this." [81]

36. *Prosopopoeia* bestows human characteristics on general notions and abstract ideas. On November 25, 1963, Hon. Mike Mansfield of Montana used prosopopoeia when he said that in President Kennedy's death man will find "the strength to do what must be done to bridle the bigotry, the hatred, the arrogance, the iniquities, and the inequities which marched in the boots of a gathering tyranny to that moment of horror." [82] On December

11, 1963, Hon. Herbert S. Walters of Tennessee stated "that when poisonous thoughts and hatred mate, they give birth to a despicable action." [83]

37. *Pysma* is a series of rhetorical questions demanding a silent answer from the hearers. For example, when speaking on "The Sublime Issue of the Work of Religion," Gregory T. Bedell asked,

> How am I to give you any information as to the intrinsic character of the happiness of heaven? Is not this something beyond the conception of man? Are we told sufficiently about it in the Scriptures to authorize speculation? Is there any thing beyond a glimpse? [84]

In his sermon on "The Bible in an Atomic Age" the Rev. Charles M. Crowe asked: "Why all this interest in the Bible in an atomic age? What chance has the Bible today? Is it out of date? What can it do for us and our world?" [85]

38. *Reduplication* is the exact restatement for emphasis. For instance, on September 6, 1780, when attempting to vindicate himself before his estranged constituents, Edmund Burke said, "Applaud us when we run; console us when we fall; cheer us when we recover; but let us pass on—for God's sake, let us pass on." [86] On December 11, 1963, Hon. Mike Mansfield of Montana stated:

> There was a sound of laughter; in a moment, it was no more. And so she [Mrs. John F. Kennedy] took a ring from her finger and placed it in his [President John F. Kennedy's] hands.
>
> There was a wit in a man neither young nor old, but a wit full of an old man's wisdom and of a child's wisdom, and then, in a moment it was no more. And so she took a ring from her finger and placed it in his hands.
>
> There was a man marked with the scars of his love of country, a body active with the surge of a life far, far from spent and, in a moment, it was no more. And so she took a ring from her finger and placed it in his hands.
>
> There was a father with a little boy, a little girl and a joy of each in the other. In a moment it was no more, and so she took a ring from her finger and placed it in his hands.[87]

39. *Simile* is a similarity between two objects directly expressed by such words as "like," "as," "as if," and "so." For example, on February 24, 1761, James Otis argued that "a Man's house is his castle; and whilst he is quiet, he is as well guarded as a prince in his castle." [88] On September 18, 1893, Booker T. Washington argued that "In all things purely social we [Negroes and Caucasians] can be as separate as the fingers, yet one as the hand in all things essential to mutual progress." [89] In his sermon

on "Jesus' Ethical Message Confronts the World," Dr. Harry Emerson Fosdick stated:

> Like children's sand houses built upon the shore, age after age the tides of destiny have risen and wiped out the empires built on force. Of all contrasts in history none could be more disproportionate than that between the Roman Empire on one side and Calvary's cross upon the other. Yet the Roman Empire has fallen and many another empire since, like children's blocks toppling in a row, but still that cross stands and haunts the conscience of the world.[90]

On April 19, 1951, before a joint meeting of the Senate and the House of Representatives, General Douglas MacArthur stated:

> I still remember the refrain of one of the most popular barrack ballads of that day which proclaimed most proudly that – 'Old soldiers never die; they just fade away.' And like the old soldier of that ballad, I now close my military career and just fade away – an old soldier who tried to do his duty as God gave him the light to see that duty.[91]

40. *Synesthesia* is the concurrent response of two or more of the senses to the stimulation of one. That is, the speaker describes one kind of sensation in terms of another. One might describe sounds in terms of colors, as a "blue note"; or colors in terms of temperature, as a "torrid green" or a "cool blue." Henry Parry Liddon once stated that "the soul *speaks* through the *eye*, which misleads us less often." [92]

41. *Synonymy* is the paraphrasing of a previous statement. This figure is illustrated by Abraham Lincoln's contention which reads:

> this government cannot endure, permanently half *slave* and half *free*. . . . I do not expect the Union to be *dissolved* – I do not expect the house to *fall* – but I *do* expect it will cease to be divided. It will become *all* one thing or *all* the other.[93]

In his sermon on "The Proper Study of Mankind," the Rev. Lynn Harold Hough stated that "Thales noticed that water could be soft and flowing. It could be hard as ice. It could vanish as vapor. In other words . . . it was a solid and a liquid and a gas." [94]

By no means should preachers labor over how many techniques they can use in a given discourse. It is far better to concentrate on the understanding and application of a few, or even a single stylistic device to achieve one's purpose for speaking. As stated earlier, figures of speech must be functional. Their primary task is to reinforce thought. They must never stand as substitutes for reason!

C. *Freshness in expression.* Style also becomes impressive through fresh expressions. A fresh expression is the direct and spontaneous expression of a person who has thought for himself, and who reveals his thoughts through language that generally is free from clichés. Clichés are expressions that once glittered but now are faded. Instead of being sprightly and vitalizing, clichés are stale and impoverished. Much of what emanates from the pulpit is a tissue of trite expression, the most pernicious being worn-out similes, hackneyed phrases, and too-familiar quotations. The following examples represent only a few of the clichés that appeared in the sermons, public speeches, and discussions of contemporary clergymen:

1. *Worn-out Similes:*

Sturdy as an oak.
Hard as granite.
As sure as taxes.
Flat as a pancake.
As impenetrable as granite.
As bold as brass.
Clear as crystal.
Straight as an arrow.
Fit as a fiddle.
Sly as a fox.
As eloquent as the apostles.
Tense as a banjo string.
Slow as the sands of the hour-glass.
Empty as a beggar's wallet.

2. *Hackneyed Phrases:*

A heart of gold.
Burning the midnight oil.
A flash in the pan.
Apple of his eye.
Chip off the old block.
The more the merrier.
Only time will tell.
Too funny for words.
In a few well-chosen words.
With a lawyer's logic.
You well know.
Drifting with the tide.
Experience has told us.
Came in with a bang.
Crack of dawn.
Set the clock back.
His two cents worth.
Hit the nail on the head.
Last but not least.
We are assembled here.
The time of my life.
Inescapable conclusion.
Went into a tailspin.
Rustic simplicity.
Verbal tapestry.
Iron determination.
Pull yourself together.
Crumbling morals.

3. *Too-Familiar Quotations:*

All that glitters is not gold.
People who live in glass houses shouldn't throw stones.
All work and no play.
When the cat is away, the mouse will play.
Right from the horse's mouth.
Sadder but wiser.
Her dress showed everything but good taste.

Death brings all people back to equality.
People don't become good and wise merely by growing old.
If you listen to only one bell, you hear only one sound.
Never put your feet where you can't see the ground.
Let's kick it around some more.
Don't build your pyramids upon needle points.
He went through a lot of trouble to be misinformed.
After God's judgment there is no court of appeals.
A man must take the fat with the lean.
Better men than I have said so.
Salvation is more than a fire escape.

No speaker can avoid all common expressions, nor should he attempt to do so; for when a cliché is "tailor-made" for a certain context, the cliché may appear bright and perceptive. The speaker should carefully examine ready-made expressions that easily come to mind, and he should employ them only if they are essential for the clear and impressive development of thought.

One final word is necessary for acquiring fresh expressions. Monotony is sleep inducing, and a monotonous vocabulary can lull people to sleep. But the speaker should never avoid an individual word because it seems simple and common. At times variations are both irritating and confusing. If the repetition of a word is vital to one's context, then repeat the word! If repetition is not essential to effective communication, then synonyms should be employed.

In conclusion, the thesis of this chapter is that the tie between context and form, between the conceptual process and expression, should never be broken. The preacher's style should always be a functional style.

6
Delivery

EACH HUMAN BEING has certain physical components that make of his voice a unique vocal instrument. While the voice is the instrument of speech, it is not the most important instrument of persuasion. Many influential speakers have vocal qualities that are not especially pleasing to the ear, but they are effective because of other elements of speech, such as the inventive or substantive factors of discourse. It is more important that the speaker concern himself with the coordination between the intellect and voice than with an excessive preoccupation to improve his voice for the sake of beauty. The clergyman or preacher, in particular, wishes to inspire his hearers to deeper commitment, not merely to entertain them with the vocal arts.

However, there are some psychological factors that relate to voice. Personality characteristics sometimes manifest themselves to audiences through the vocal presentation. A dynamic personality is apt to produce greater volume, a faster rate, and inflectional variety. An introvertive personality may have suppressive effects on vocal components. One's mental attitude during the preparation and at the time of delivery of a speech usually is conveyed through the voice and received by the listener. These considerations are very personal matters. Each preacher receives feedback or can seek it from his congregation to get an estimate of how others perceive him while they are listening. Each preacher must determine for himself whether these considerations constitute major obstacles to his communicative effectiveness.

VOCAL PRESENTATIONS

An understanding of rate, volume, pitch, quality, pronunciation, and articulation as isolated variables affecting the vocal act is desirable. The preacher should be aware, however, that a vocal problem may involve more than one of these variables, and that one variable may relate to others. For example, a very rapid rate of speech may cause slovenly articulation and a lack of inflectional variety. A clergyman who suspects that he has a vocal problem should consult personnel formally educated in speech. Self-analysis by the clergyman or by people unfamiliar with voice problems usually leads to a mistaken diagnosis and hence results in no improvement.

1. *Rate.* The number of words one delivers during a given period of time can easily be calculated. Simply read aloud a passage of prose, and time the passage in seconds. Count the number of words in the passage, divide by the number of seconds, and multiply this result by sixty to calculate the number of words per minute. This statistic alone takes on meaning only when it is analyzed within a specific context. Most people speak within a range of 140 to 160 words per minute. This does not mean that if the clergyman speaks at a rate of ninety words per minute he is speaking too slowly, nor that he speaks too rapidly if his rate is two hundred words a minute. The ultimate test of a desirable rate for each communicator is whether or not the listener comprehends the message.

One misconception about rate of delivery is that one must speak slowly in order that the listeners may comprehend what is being said. For instance, a speaker may talk so slowly that his hearers become bored. The clergyman must realize that listening is a silent process and that the mind is capable of comprehending large quantities of stimuli. The process of reading is a silent process in which the mind can comprehend far more than the oral average of 140 to 160 words per minute. Hence, it is not the number of words per minute that alone dictates a desirable rate.

The pause is another effective tool in the speaking situation. It can be planned consciously in the preparation of the sermon. The pause may emphasize partition between main points or any major divisional units of discourse. For example, the preacher may plan to pause after completing the introduction of his sermon. The pause is comparable to the transitional statement, in that it gives the hearer a brief chance to reflect on what was said and to prepare for what is to be said. The preacher may write on his notes where he plans to pause in his sermon or other public speeches. The effect of pause on any rate of delivery should be favorable in that it disallows a monotonous stream or pattern of delivery. Another misconception is that the speaker must continuously fill the air with sounds. This leads to the undesirable practice of filling pauses with the sound "uh." It is better to use the silent pause than to let the "uhs" intrude and draw attention to themselves.

2. *Volume.* Preachers often inherit churches that are not designed for human discourse. Fortunate are men who become involved with the building of a new church and can recommend that attention be given to the acoustical nature of the interior.

Many clergymen face the problem of having to adapt to the size of a church so that they may be heard by all members of the audience. The microphone has become a remarkable help, and it should be used if members of the audience complain that they are unable to hear the speaker. However, some clergymen think that they must shout into the microphone in order to be heard. The microphone, if set up with an adequate amplifying system, is a very delicate instrument. One of the major qualities of electronic media is intimacy; the clergyman may speak as though he were holding an interpersonal dialogue with one member of the congregation. If a speaker finds it necessary to shout into the microphone, it may well be that the electronic system is inadequate for the size of the church, or it is possible that the interior of the church needs acoustical treatment.

If the preacher does not use a microphone, he may have to work to ensure that he is heard by everyone. He should practice keeping his chin up and looking at those farthest away, so that his sounds are physically projected to the audience and not to the notes he may be using. He should also develop careful habits of articulation so that his words are intelligible to the hearers.

3. *Pitch.* Because of social expectations, people tend to respond unfavorably to highly pitched sounds emanating from male speakers. However, some male speakers who have highly

pitched voices are effective communicators because they are able to concentrate on other skills of discourse so successfully that high pitch no longer draws attention to itself. Analysis by a qualified person can assist such speakers.

Monopitch or monotone is another factor to consider, for preachers can lose the full semantic context of their messages if they habitually speak in monotones. It is not uncommon for preachers to speak in a monotone from the pulpit even when they do not do so in their private conversations. In every form of discourse the clergyman should coordinate the pitch of his voice with his *ideas;* ideas alone should determine the vocal mode.

4. *Quality.* Each person has his own unique quality of voice. It is common to identify a person merely by his voice. Research reveals that no matter what distinct quality a voice has, listeners become acclimated to it after hearing it a number of times. The listener tends to adjust to a quality and thereafter identifies it as a normal characteristic of the particular person. Even though a preacher has a distracting quality of voice, it will not necessarily call attention to itself when the hearers become familiar with it.

5. *Pronunciation.* Like most respected leaders in society, speakers are expected to employ pronunciation that meets the standards of well-educated people. Pronunciation involves choice in uttering sounds and stressing words in such a way that the words do not call attention to themselves. The preacher should be concerned with communicating the concepts of his sermon and naturally would be disconcerted to discover that his congregation was discussing his pronunciation of words rather than the concepts of his sermon. Therefore, it is advisable that he rehearse the proper pronunciation of words until he uses them without having to think about them. Some of the more notorious words mispronounced by preachers are "jist" for "just"; "goin'" for "going"; "git" for "get"; and "ta" for "to." Clergymen would be wise to follow standard references of pronunciation when preparing their sermons.

6. *Articulation.* Whereas pronunciation essentially involves human choice as to the ways sounds are uttered and words stressed, articulation involves human capacity to reproduce vowels and consonants so that they are intelligible to the hearer.

Most clergymen are capable of producing the forty-four primary sounds of the English language, but careless habits develop if some attention is not given to articulation. One method is to request someone to sit in the seat farthest from the pulpit and to check for articulatory effectiveness. Another method is to listen to oneself over a tape recorder. A third method is to practice a sermon in church by speaking without phonation. This is the act of whispering so that the vocal bands are not vibrating and thus producing sounds. While speaking without phonation the preacher may concentrate on clearly enunciating the vowels and consonants to increase intelligibility. Moreover, a preacher should occasionally invite someone formally trained in speech to analyze his vocal characteristics. It may well be that such a trained critic can suggest changes for more effective communication.

VISUAL PRESENTATIONS

Ancient and contemporary viewers and critics of public speaking have revealed great sensitivity to the ways in which speakers conduct themselves while proceeding to, standing and walking on, and withdrawing from the platform. Several examples should illustrate this observation.

In his *Brutus* Cicero praised Antonius because "his gesture did not seek to reflect words, but agreed with the course of his thought – hands, shoulders, chest, stamp of the foot, posture in repose and in movement, all harmonizing with his words and thoughts." [1] This source also reveals that, because Curio awkwardly swayed his body while speaking, Gaius Julius Caesar Strabo asked, "Who is the fellow there talking from a skiff?" [2] And Gnaeus Sicinius said to Curio's colleague, Octavius: "You can never thank your colleague enough, Octavius; for if he had not thrashed about in his way, the flies would surely have eaten you alive right here and now." [3]

In 1644 John Bulwer issued his *Chirologia . . . and Chironomia* which treated approximately 170 analyses and canons of the gestures of the hands and fingers. This detailed work served as the basis of many subsequent treatises, and as a rationale of the whole subject of gesture.

In 1852 Chauncey Goodrich, Professor of Rhetoric at Yale from 1817 to 1839, published *Select British Eloquence,* a rhe-

torical analysis of twenty-one orators. In his work Goodrich remarked that William Pitt's "gesture was animated, but devoid of grace";[4] that Edmund Burke's "gait and gesture were awkward";[5] that Thomas Erskine was "animated and graceful in gesture, with . . . an eye of piercing keenness and power";[6] and that Charles James Fox "stood on the floor of the House like a Norfolkshire farmer in the midst of his fellows; short, thick-set, with his broad shoulders and capacious chest, his bushy hair and eyebrows, and his dark countenance working with emotion, the very image of blunt and honesty."[7]

The well-known volumes of *A History and Criticism of American Public Address,* prepared under the auspices of The Speech Association of America (1955-1960), reveal detailed analyses of the mannerisms of Jonathan Edwards, Theodore S. Parker, Henry Ward Beecher, Phillips Brooks, Wendell Phillips, Robert G. Ingersoll, Henry W. Grady, Booker T. Washington, Rufus Choate, Jeremiah S. Black, William M. Evarts, Ralph Waldo Emerson, Charles W. Eliot, Edwin A. Alderman, Samuel Gompers, Patrick Henry, Henry Clay, John C. Calhoun, Daniel Webster, William L. Yancey, Charles Sumner, Stephen A. Douglas, Abraham Lincoln, James G. Blaine, William Jennings Bryan, Albert J. Beveridge, Robert M. La Follette, Woodrow Wilson, Alexander Hamilton, Thomas Hart Benton, Susan B. Anthony, George William Curtis, Lucius Q. C. Lamar, Dwight L. Moody, Clarence Darrow, Theodore Roosevelt, William E. Borah, Harry Emerson Fosdick, and Franklin Delano Roosevelt.

The visual presentations of today's preachers are not exempt from criticism. This fact is evidenced by the following quotations that represent only a few of the hundreds of criticisms which parishioners of various denominations offered in reply to the authors' questions about the physical mannerisms of their pulpiteers. The criticisms pertain to the individual preacher's mannerisms while proceeding to, standing and moving on, and withdrawing from the pulpit or platform. The names of the clergymen alluded to in the criticisms have been deleted from this text.

Criticisms Aimed at the Preacher's Posture:

"Father ________ looks sloppy, the way he slouches so much."

"Reverend ________ looks lazy and bored because he leans on the pulpit."

"Reverend ________ looks rather silly standing at rigid attention."

"Father ________ always seems to stand with his feet spread far apart and his hands on his hips. He looks as though he is ready to take on the whole congregation."

"Reverend ________ always has his head drooping. I sure wish he'd look at us once in a while."

Criticisms Aimed at the Preacher's Eye Contact with the Audience:

"Rabbi ________ constantly looks at the floor or ceiling."

"I, too, began to stare at the ceiling. I kept wondering what was up there. Looks like Father ________ is afraid to look at us."

"Reverend ________ bores me to death. He seems so arrogant the way he ignores us. If he took his nose out of his notes I might listen to him. I usually sleep when he talks."

Criticisms Aimed at the Preacher's Movements:

"Reverend ________ walks too slow; he lulls me to sleep."

"Reverend ________ walks too quickly. He appears to be over anxious in getting to the pulpit to 'get the darned old sermon over with.' "

"Father makes me laugh whenever he walks. He looks like he is sneaking out of the house. He should quit walking on tiptoes."

"I think Father ________ is a pompous ass! I don't think he knows we are present, the way he sticks his chest out and his head up so high."

"I sometimes get woozy from watching Rabbi ________. Why, it's ridiculous the way he sways back and forth. My old speech teacher would probably want to nail his shoes to the floor. He did that to me once and I learned quickly."

"Oh, most of the time Father ________ does a fine job. The only thing I don't like is that he begins to talk before he gets to the pulpit and returns to the altar while concluding his sermon. This distracts my concentration on what he says."

Criticisms Aimed at the Preacher's Facial Expressions:

"Father ________ is a dud. He keeps the same dead-pan expression throughout his speeches. It's difficult to warm up to his ideas."

"Reverend ________ means well but looks ridiculous by trying to find a facial expression for everything he says. A few emphatic ones would be much better than so damned many silly ones."

"Rabbi ________ just doesn't move me. He never seems to be shook up over anything he says. It doesn't matter if he talks seriously or funny; he always looks the same. I'm glad he's going back in the Navy."

Criticisms Aimed at the Preacher's Gestures:

"Reverend ________'s gestures are clumsy. They lack timing and are too jerky. Just raising an arm a little doesn't do anything for his speech."

"Reverend ________'s gestures look mechanical. In speech class I learned that gestures and movements should be natural. Reverend ________ looks like he planned all of his."

"I always thought clergymen were underpaid. Father ________ looks like he's proud of his money. He's always jingling his coins while he speaks."

"I only wish that the Rabbi would quit fiddling with his watch. He looks so nervous he makes me feel edgy at times."

"Father ________ is always cracking his knuckles."

"Maybe someday the suspenders of Reverend ________ will break. He always pulls on them when he speaks."

"Fingernails should be treated at home; not in the pulpit."

"Speeches should be planned beforehand. Father ________ always has to arrange his notes in the pulpit."

"I wish he would put those notes away. He always shuffles them while speaking."

"I learned to put off golf on Sunday morning, but I'll go back to the greens if I have to listen to some boring speaker who constantly picks his nose."

"What annoys me is Father's constant rubbing of his beard. So he's got a beard. Big deal! What does his beard have to do with his talks on moral principles?"

Criticisms Aimed at the Preacher's Use of Audiovisual Aids:

"I sat to the side of the room and never did see Father's charts."

"I couldn't read the lettering. Father should have used a darker background."

"Reverend ________'s letters were too small."

"When Father no longer needed his picture of the accident, he should have put it away. Too many of us kept looking at the picture. I missed much of what followed."

"I was quite attentive until Reverend ________ passed out the pictures. Then I started to watch the people's reaction to the pictures and didn't listen to what he was saying."

"The volume was too high. I got a headache from the loud noise. The acoustics were terrible."

The preceding statements reveal that certain visual presentations of the clergy are not conducive to effective communication. The public is evidently aware of these liabilities and is not reluctant to criticize a speaker just because he is in a pulpit. For these reasons preachers should adhere to the following dicta.

First, speakers must establish and maintain eye contact with their audiences. Eye contact generates emotional appeal. By looking directly at the audience, the speaker makes his hearers feel wanted. People who attend church services expect to hear speeches, not soliloquies; and effective communication calls for identification between the speaker and his audience. Why should anyone listen to a speaker who fails to acknowledge the presence of the listeners? Eye contact also is helpful to the speaker in that it allows for feedback. Feedback is the process whereby the speaker receives gestural or verbal signals emanating intentionally or unintentionally from the audience. Feedback enables the speaker to evaluate his communicative effectiveness as he is speaking. Thus, feedback may inform the speaker that he is confusing his hearers by progressing too rapidly, or is boring them by going too slowly. Finally, eye contact with the audience enhances the speaker's *ethos*. Goodwill is shown when the speaker shows his interest in his audience. Character is connoted by the speaker's firmness and confidence. A speaker who cannot look directly at his audience usually displays fear; fear displays weakness; and weakness usually is incompatible with character. Moreover, intelligence is shown when the speaker is not dependent on note cards. By freely looking at the audience, the speaker demonstrates that he has mastered his subject and has prepared his presentation.

Probably one of the best explanations of the value of feedback comes from Booker T. Washington. In his autobiography Washington said:

> If in an audience . . . there is one person who is not in sympathy with my views, or is inclined to be doubtful, cold, or critical, I can pick him out. When I have found him I usually go straight at him, and it is a great satisfaction to watch the process of his thawing out.[8]

Not only did feedback inform Washington when his audience disagreed with him, but also it enlightened him when he was affecting them favorably. For example, Washington remarked:

> There is great compensation . . . that comes to me after I have been speaking for about ten minutes, and have come to feel that I have really mastered my audience, and that we have gotten into full and complete sympathy with each other. It seems to me that there is rarely such a combination of mental and physical delight in any effort as that which comes to a public speaker when he feels that he has a great audience completely within his control. There is a thread of sympathy and oneness that connects a public speaker with his audience, that is just as strong as though it was something tangible and visible.[9]

Washington's remarks clearly reveal the necessity of establishing and maintaining eye contact with one's audience.

The second dictum is that the preacher's movements and gestures must be natural, not planned. When used appropriately, movements aid the speaker in several ways. Movements help to release tension in the legs and stomach. Movements help to emphasize an idea. For instance, by taking a step forward when saying, "Now this is important," the speaker strengthens his point. Movements also prevent monotony. A speaker who remains in one position for too long a period often lulls his hearers to sleep. Movements also help to establish direct contact with all members of the audience. Then, too, movements serve as transitions. For example, by taking a step after concluding a particular topic, the speaker enables himself and his hearers to prepare for the next topic. Finally, movements aid in heightening the speaker's confidence and poise. By not having to lean on or stand behind a rostrum or pulpit, the speaker is free to maintain directness and strengthen his audience rapport.

To accomplish the above advantages, the speaker's movements must be natural and functional. To be functional means that the movements coordinate with the speaker's ideas. The movements must draw attention to the speaker's thoughts, not to themselves. This demands that the movements be natural; they must not be rehearsed; they must come only from the heart. The clergy would be wise to adhere to the idea of Thomas Sheridan, who said:

> When we reflect that the end of public speaking is persuasion . . . and that in order to persuade others to the belief of any point, it must first appear, that the person who attempts it is firmly persuaded of the truth of it himself; how can we suppose it possible that he should affect this, unless he delivers himself in the manner which is always used by persons who speak in earnest? How shall his words pass for the words of truth, when they bear not his stamp? [10]

Gestures also are valuable aids to the speaker in that they clarify size, shape, position, or movement, and identify and reinforce feelings or attitudes. But gestures, too, must be natural and functional. Speakers would benefit if they followed Hamlet's advice to players. In Shakespeare's classic, Hamlet states: "Nor do not saw the air too much with your hand, thus; but use all gently; for in the very torrent, tempest, and as I may say, whirlwind of passion, you must acquire and beget a temperance that may give it smoothness." [11] Hamlet also states:

> Be not too tame neither, but let your own discretion be your tutor: suit the action to the word, the word to the action; with this special observance, that you o'erstep not the modesty of nature: for anything so overdone is from the purpose of playing, whose end, both at the first and now, was and is, to hold, as 'twere, the mirror up to nature.[12]

The third dictum is that speakers must coordinate their facial expressions with their ideas. Facial expressions are important because they may truly reveal the constructions of the mind. When a speaker's face is constant, when it fails to vary from one emotional appeal to another, then he appears to be indifferent to his words. If a speaker fails to appear moved by his thoughts, then why should the hearers become involved?

The last dictum for visual presentations is that preachers must be functional in their use of visual aids. The visual aids available to the clergy are many, among which are blackboards, diagrams, graphs, maps, models, pictures, films, and slides. Regardless of the kinds of visual aids used, preachers must never forget that *they* themselves are the primary aids. They must interpret their aids; they must give purpose to their materials. To do this, preachers must make certain that the aids call attention only to their own thoughts and not to the aids themselves. Hence, visual aids must always be relevant and subordinate to the thoughts under discussion, and must always be in such a position as to be seen by all members of the audience.

In conclusion, the thesis of this chapter is that the clergy's vocal and visual presentations must never call attention to themselves but must always reinforce the speaker's concepts. To be functional the vocal and visual presentations must appear natural, not rehearsed. Booker T. Washington wisely remarked:

> I do not believe that one should speak unless, deep down in his heart, he feels convinced that he has a message to deliver. When one feels, from the bottom of his feet to the top of his head, that he has something to say that is going to help some individual or some cause, then let him say it. . . . When I have an address to deliver, I like to forget all about the rules for the proper use of the English language, and all about rhetoric and that sort of thing, and I like to make the audience forget all about these things, too.[13]

To be an effective speaker is difficult. The speaker needs to know a sufficient amount of rhetorical theory, and must be able to apply the theory in a manner that calls attention only to the speaker's ideas. This text has endeavored to supply the needed theory for the busy clergy. The clergy must now apply it.

Appendix 1
Sources of Material for Sermons and Speeches

A. Journals, Newspapers, Magazines, Reviews, Bulletins, and Newsletters:

Adult Leadership
The American Baptist Chaplain
American Historical Review
American Journal of Philology
American Journal of Psychology
American Journal of Sociology
American Political Science Review
American Scholar
American Sociological Review
The Atlantic
Baptist Leader
Behavioral Science
The Biblical Archaeologist
Catholic Herald-Citizen
Challenge, the Magazine of Economic Affairs
The Christian Century
Christian Rural Fellowship Bulletin
Christianity and Crisis
Church Administration
Church in Metropolis
City Church
Commonweal
Concern
Consumer Reports
Current History
Ebony
Focus Midwest
Foreign Affairs
Foundations: A Baptist Journal of History & Theology
Harper's Magazine
Harvard Business Review
Harvard Theological Review
Here and Now
Information Service of the Lutheran World Federation
Spectrum (International Journal of Religious Education)
The Jewish Quarterly Review
Journal of Biblical Literature
Journal of Near Eastern Studies
Life
Look
Mind
Mission
Modern Philology
Motive
Newsweek
The New York Times
Pastor (New Christian Advocate)
Pastoral Psychology
Philosophical Review
Psychology Today
Public Opinion Quarterly
The Pulpit
Reader's Digest
The Review of Metaphysics
The Review of Politics
Rural Missions
Saturday Review
Scientific American
Social Forces
Time

Town & Country Church
United Church Herald
U. S. News and World Report
Vietnam Perspectives
Vital Speeches of the Day
The Washington Post
Yale Review
Your Church

B. Books:

Andrews, F. Emerson, *Attitudes Toward Giving.* New York: Russell Sage Foundation, 1953.

Ayres, Francis D., *The Ministry of the Laity.* Philadelphia: The Westminster Press, 1962.

Bainton, Roland H., *Christian Attitudes toward War and Peace.* Nashville: Abingdon Press, 1960.

________________, *What Christianity Says about Sex, Love, and Marriage.* New York: Association Press, 1957.

Baker, Oren Huling, *Human Nature under God.* New York: Association Press, 1958.

Baker, Wesley C., *The Split-Level Fellowship.* Philadelphia: The Westminster Press, 1965.

Batchelder, Alan B., *The Economics of Poverty.* New York: John Wiley and Sons, Inc., 1966.

Beckert, Ernest, *The Structure of Evil.* New York: George Braziller, Inc., 1968.

Bekkers, W. M., *God's People on the March.* New York: Holt, Rinehart & Winston, Inc., 1966.

Benko, Stephen, *Protestants, Catholics, and Mary.* Valley Forge: The Judson Press, 1968.

Bernstein, Saul, *Alternatives to Violence.* New York: Association Press, 1967.

________________, *Youth on the Streets.* New York: Association Press, 1964.

Bibby, Cyril, *Race, Prejudice and Education.* New York: Frederick. A. Praeger, Inc., 1957.

Blanshard, Paul, *God and Man in Washington.* Boston: Beacon Press, 1960.

Bonhoeffer, Dietrich, *Life Together.* New York: Harper & Row, Publishers, Inc., 1954.

Bonnell, John Sutherland, *No Escape from Life.* New York: Harper & Row, Publishers, Inc. 1958.

Borsodi, Ralph, *This Ugly Civilization.* New York: Simon and Schuster, Inc., 1929.

Bosworth, Allan R., *America's Concentration Camps.* New York: W. W. Norton & Company, Inc., 1967.

Boulding, Kenneth E., *The Meaning of the Twentieth Century.* New York: Harper & Row, Publishers, Inc., 1964.

Bouman, LeRoy, *The American Funeral.* New York: Paperback Library, Inc., 1959.

Bovet, Theodore, *Love, Skill and Mystery.* Garden City: Doubleday & Company, Inc., 1958.

Boyd, Malcolm, *Are You Running with Me, Jesus?* New York: Holt, Rinehart & Winston, Inc., 1965.

________________, ed., *On the Battle Lines.* New York: Morehouse-Barlow Co., Inc., 1964.

Bradley, William L., *The Meaning of Christian Values Today.* Philadelphia: The Westminster Press, 1964.

Brattgard, Helge, *God's Stewards.* Minneapolis: Augsburg Publishing House, 1963.

Brink, William and Harris, Louis, *Black and White.* New York: Simon and Schuster, Inc., 1966.

________________, *The Negro Revolution in America.* New York: Simon and Schuster, Inc., 1964.

Broderick, Francis L. and Meier, August, *Negro Protest Thought in the Twentieth Century.* Indianapolis: The Bobbs-Merrill Company, Inc., 1965.

Broholm, Richard R., *The Man of Faith in The New Age.* Valley Forge: The Judson Press, 1964.

Brown, Claude, *Manchild in the Promised Land.* New York: The Macmillan Company, 1965.

Brown, Robert R., *Bigger than Little Rock.* New York: The Seabury Press, Inc., 1958.

Burke, Carl F., *God Is for Real, Man.* New York: Association Press, 1966.

Burkhart, Roy A., *How the Church Grows.* New York: Harper & Row, Publishers, Inc., 1947.

Cappon, Daniel, *Toward an Understanding of Homosexuality.* Englewood Cliffs: Prentice-Hall, Inc., 1965.

Cate, William B., *The Ecumenical Scandal on Main Street.* New York: Association Press, 1965.

Chastain, Theron, *We Can Win Others.* Valley Forge: The Judson Press, 1953.

Clark, Henry, *The Christian Case Against Poverty.* New York: Association Press, 1965.

Clark, Kenneth B., *Dark Ghetto.* New York: Harper & Row, Publishers, Inc., 1965.

________________, *The Negro Protest.* Boston: Beacon Press, 1963.

Clebsch, William A., *From Sacred to Profane America.* New York: Harper & Row, Publishers, Inc., 1968.

Conant, James B., *Slums and Suburbs.* New York: McGraw-Hill Inc., 1961.

Conrad, Earl, *The Invention of The Negro.* New York: Paul S. Eriksson, Inc., 1966.

Cook, Fred J., *The FBI Nobody Knows.* New York: The Macmillan Company, 1964.

Cornell, George W., *The Way and Its Ways.* New York: Association Press, 1963.

Cox, Harvey, *God's Revolution and Man's Responsibility.* Valley Forge: The Judson Press, 1965.

Cross, Robert D., ed., *The Church and the City,* Indianapolis: The Bobbs-Merrill Company, Inc., 1966.

Cubbedge, Robert E., *Who Needs People?* Washington, D.C.: Robert B. Luce, Inc., 1963.

Cuber, John F. and Harroff, Peggy B., *The Significant Americans.* New York: Appleton-Century, 1965.

Davies, Horton, *The Challenge of the Sects.* Philadelphia: The Westminster Press, 1954.

Davis, John P., ed., *The American Negro Reference Book*. Englewood Cliffs: Prentice-Hall, Inc., 1965.
Dawson, Christopher, *The Movement of World Revolution*. New York: Sheed & Ward, Inc., 1959.
Dobriner, William M., *Class in Suburbia*. Englewood Cliffs: Prentice-Hall, Inc., 1963.
Dolan, Rex R., *The Big Change*. Philadelphia: The Westminster Press, 1967.
Duncan, Hugh, *Symbols in Society*. New York: Oxford University Press, Inc., 1968.
Erikson, Erik H., *Insight and Responsibility*. New York: W. W. Norton & Company, Inc., 1964.
Felton, Ralph A., *The Pulpit and the Plow*. New York: Friendship Press, 1960.
Ferre, Nels, F. S., *Making Religion Real*. New York: Harper & Row Publishers, Inc., 1955.
Flesch, Rudolph, *Art of Plaintalk*. New York: Harper & Row, Publishers, Inc., 1946.
Fletcher, Joseph, *Situation Ethics*. Philadelphia: The Westminster Press, 1966.
Frellick, Francis I., *Helping Youth in Conflict*. Englewood Cliffs: Prentice-Hall, Inc., 1964.
Friedan, Betty, *The Feminine Mystique*. New York: W. W. Norton & Company, Inc., 1963.
Fromm, Erich, *The Art of Loving*. New York: Harper & Row, Publishers, Inc., 1956.
Galbraith, John Kenneth, *The Affluent Society*. Boston: Houghton Mifflin Company, 1958.
Giallombardo, Rose, ed., *Juvenile Delinquency*. New York: John Wiley & Sons, Inc., 1966.
Gibbs, Mark and Morton, T. Ralph, *God's Frozen People – A Book for and about Christian Laymen*. Philadelphia: The Westminster Press, 1964.
Gilmore, A., *Baptism and Christian Unity*. Valley Forge: The Judson Press, 1966.
Ginzberg, Eli, *Values and Ideas of American Youth*. New York: Columbia University Press, 1961.
Goldstein, Joseph and Katz, Jay, *The Family and the Law*. New York: The Free Press, 1965.
Goodman, Paul, *Growing Up Absurd*. New York: Random House, Inc., 1960.
Gordon, Albert I., *Jews in Suburbia*. Boston: Beacon Press, 1959.
Gordon, Mitchell, *Sick Cities*. New York: The Macmillan Company, 1963.
Gornitzka, A. Reuben, *Who Cares?* Westwood: Fleming H. Revell Co., 1966.
Grambs, Jean Dresden, *Schools, Scholars, and Society*. Englewood Cliffs: Prentice-Hall, Inc., 1965.
Gran, John, *Why Children Become Delinquent*. Baltimore: Helicon Press, Inc., 1961.
Green, Constance McLaughlin, *The Secret City*. Princeton: Princeton University Press, 1967.

Gruen, Victor, *The Heart of Our Cities.* New York: Simon and Schuster, Inc., 1964.

Guilbaud, G. T., *What Is Cybernetics?* New York: Grove Press, Inc., 1960.

Guzzardi, Walter, Jr., *The Young Executives.* New York: The New American Library, Inc., 1965.

Halvorson, Loren E., *Exodus into the World.* Minneapolis: Augsburg Publishing House, 1966.

Handlin, Oscar, *The Newcomers.* Cambridge: Harvard University Press, 1959.

Harris, Sara, *Hell-Hole.* New York: E. P. Dutton & Co., 1967.

Harrison, Paul M., *Authority and Power in the Free Church Tradition.* Princeton: Princeton University Press, 1959.

Heilbroner, Robert L., *The Limits of American Capitalism.* New York: Harper & Row, Publishers, Inc., 1965.

Herberg, Will, *Protestant-Catholic-Jew.* New York: Doubleday & Company, Inc., 1955.

Higbee, Edward, *The Squeeze.* New York: William Morrow & Co., Inc., 1960.

Hodnett, Edward, *The Cultivated Mind.* New York: Harper & Row, Publishers, Inc., 1963.

Hostetler, John A., *Amish Society.* Baltimore: The Johns Hopkins Press, 1963.

Hull, Eleanor, *The Church Not Made with Hands.* Valley Forge: The Judson Press, 1965.

Jackson, Edgar N., *The Christian Funeral.* New York: Channel Press, 1966.

________________, *For the Living.* New York: Channel Press, 1964.

Jones, Richard M., *The Man for All Men.* Valley Forge: The Judson Press, 1965.

Jourard, Sidney M., *The Transparent Self.* Princeton: D. Van Nostrand Co., Inc., 1964.

Jung, Carl G., *Man and His Symbols.* New York: Doubleday and Company, 1964.

Jurji, Edward J., ed., *The Ecumenical Era in Church and Society.* New York: The Macmillan Company, 1959.

Kahn, Herman and Wiener, Anthony J., *The Year 2000.* New York: The Macmillan Company, 1967.

Keech, William J., *The Life I Owe.* Valley Forge: The Judson Press, 1963.

Keil, Charles, *Urban Blues.* Chicago: The University of Chicago Press, 1966.

King, Martin Luther, Jr., *Why We Can't Wait.* New York: Harper & Row, Publishers, Inc., 1963.

Kitagawa, Daisuke, *The Pastor and the Race Issue.* New York: The Seabury Press, Inc., 1965.

Klein, Woody, *Let In the Sun.* New York: The Macmillan Company, 1964.

Koestler, Arthur, *The Act of Creation.* New York: The Macmillan Company, 1964.

Kozol, Jonathan, *Death at an Early Age.* Boston: Houghton Mifflin Company, 1967.

Kulski, Julian Eugene, *Land of Urban Promise*. Notre Dame: University of Notre Dame Press, 1966.

Latourette, Kenneth Scott, *The Christian Outlook*. New York: Harper & Row, Publishers, Inc., 1948.

Lincoln, C. Eric, *The Black Muslims in America*. Boston: Beacon Press, 1961.

Linn, Edmund H., *Preaching as Counseling*. Valley Forge: The Judson Press, 1966.

Litwack, Leon F., *North of Slavery*. Chicago: University of Chicago Press, 1961.

Longgood, William, *Poisons in Your Food*. New York: Simon and Schuster, Inc., 1960.

Lorenz, Konrad, *On Aggression*. New York: Harcourt, Brace & World, Inc., 1966.

Loth, David, *Crime in the Suburbs*. New York: William Morrow & Co., Inc., 1967.

Lowe, Jeanne, *Cities in a Race with Time*. New York: Random House, Inc., 1967.

Luckmann, Thomas, *The Invisible Religion*. New York: The Macmillan Company, 1967.

Luecke, Richard, *New Meanings for New Beings*. Philadelphia: Fortress Press, 1964.

Malinowski, Bronislaw, *Sex, Culture and Myth*. New York: Harcourt, Brace & World, Inc., 1962.

Marrow, Alfred J., *Changing Patterns of Prejudice*. Philadelphia: Chilton Company, 1962.

Marty, Martin E., *Babylon by Choice*. New York: Friendship Press, 1965.

Marvin, Ernest, *Odds Against Evens*. Philadelphia: The Westminster Press, 1968.

Matthews, Stanley G., *The Night Pastors*. New York: Hawthorn Books, Inc., 1967.

May, Edgar, *The Wasted Americans*. New York: Harper & Row, Publishers, Inc., 1964.

McLaughlin, Henry, *The Gospel in Action*. Richmond: John Knox Press, 1944.

Mendelson, Wallace, *Discrimination*. Englewood Cliffs: Prentice-Hall, Inc., 1962.

Mercer, Blaine E., *The American Community*. New York: Random House, Inc., 1956.

Miller, Randolph Crump, *Youth Considers Parents as People*. Camden: Thomas Nelson & Sons, 1965.

Mills, C. Wright, *Images of Man*. New York: George Braziller, Inc., 1960.

Mitford, Jessica, *The American Way of Death*. New York: Simon and Schuster, Inc., 1963.

Moomaw, I. W., *To Hunger No More*. New York: Friendship Press, 1963.

Moore, Paul, Jr., *The Church Reclaims the City*. New York: The Seabury Press, Inc., 1963.

Moskin, J. Robert, *Morality in America*. New York: Random House, Inc., 1966.

Mumford, Lewis, *The Myth of the Machine.* New York: Harcourt, Brace & World, Inc., 1967.
Munby, D. L., *God and the Rich Society.* New York: Oxford University Press, Inc., 1961.
Murray, Edward J., *Motivation and Emotion.* Englewood Cliffs: Prentice-Hall, Inc., 1964.
Niebuhr, Reinhold, *Man's Nature and His Communities.* New York: Charles Scribner's Sons, 1965.
Oden, Thomas C., *Contemporary Theology and Psychotherapy.* Philadelphia: The Westminster Press, 1967.
Olson, Bernhard E., *Faith and Prejudice.* New Haven: Yale University Press, 1963.
Osofsky, Gilbert, *The Burden of Race.* New York: Harper & Row, Publishers, Inc., 1967.
Packard, Vance, *The Hidden Persuaders.* New York: David McKay Co., Inc., 1957.
—————, *The Naked Society.* New York: David McKay Co., Inc., 1964.
—————, *The Waste Makers,* New York: David McKay Co., Inc., 1960.
Perry, John D., *The Coffee House Ministry.* Richmond: John Knox Press, 1967.
Pike, James A., *You and the New Morality.* New York: Harper & Row, Publishers, Inc., 1967.
Powledge, Fred, *Black Power, White Resistance.* Cleveland: The World Publishing Company, 1967.
Powell, Luther P., *Money and the Church.* New York: Association Press, 1963.
Presthus, Robert, *Men at the Top.* New York: Oxford University Press, Inc., 1964.
Raab, Earl, ed., *American Race Relations Today.* Garden City: Doubleday & Company, Inc., 1963.
Reed, Luther D., *Worship.* Philadelphia: Fortress Press, 1959.
Reid, Clyde, *The God-Evaders.* New York: Harper & Row, Publishers, Inc., 1966.
Remmers, H. H. and Radler, D. H., *The American Teenager.* Indianapolis: The Bobbs-Merrill Company, Inc., 1957.
Riis, Jacob A., *How the Other Half Lives.* Boston: Sagamore Press, Inc., 1957.
Ritz, Joseph P., *The Despised Poor.* Boston: Beacon Press, 1966.
Robb, Thomas Bradley, *The Bonus Years.* Valley Forge: The Judson Press, 1968.
Roberts, David E., *Psychotherapy and a Christian View of Man.* New York: Charles Scribner's Sons, 1950.
Root, Robert, *Progress Against Prejudice.* New York: Friendship Press, 1957.
Rossi, Peter H., *Why Families Move.* New York: The Free Press, 1956.
Rugg, Harold, *Imagination.* New York: Harper & Row, Publishers, Inc., 1963.
Ruitenbeek, Hendrick M., ed., *The Dilemma of Organizational Society.* New York: E. P. Dutton & Co., Inc., 1963.
Sanders, Irwin T., *The Community.* New York: The Ronald Press Company, 1958.

Scotford, John R., *Church Union, Why Not?* Philadelphia: (imprint United Church Press) The Pilgrim Press, 1948.

Shedd, Charlie W., *How to Develop a Tithing Church.* Nashville: Abingdon Press, 1961.

Sherman, Harvey, *It All Depends.* University: University of Alabama Press, 1966.

Silberman, Charles E., *Crisis in Black and White.* New York: Random House, Inc., 1964.

Silver, Nathan, *Lost New York.* Boston: Houghton Mifflin Company, 1967.

Simon, Arthur, *Faces of Poverty.* St. Louis: Concordia Publishing House, 1966.

Sirjamaki, John, *The American Family in the Twentieth Century.* Cambridge: Harvard University Press, 1953.

Slocum, Walter L., *Agricultural Sociology.* New York: Harper & Row, Publishers, Inc., 1962.

Stagg, Paul L., *The Converted Church.* Valley Forge: The Judson Press, 1967.

Stein, Edward V., *Guilt: Theory and Therapy.* Philadelphia: The Westminster Press, 1968.

Stark, Rodney and Glock, Charles Y., *American Piety.* Berkeley: University of California Press, 1968.

Stringfellow, William, *Dissenter in a Great Society.* New York: Holt, Rinehart & Winston, Inc., 1966.

Thomas, Piri, *Down These Mean Streets.* New York: Alfred A. Knopf, Inc., 1967.

Tibbetts, Orlando, *The Reconciling Community.* Valley Forge: The Judson Press, 1969.

Tillich, Paul, *The Courage To Be.* New Haven: Yale University Press, 1952.

______________, *Love, Power and Justice.* New York: Oxford University Press, Inc., 1960.

Torbet, Robert G., *The Baptist Ministry—Then and Now.* Valley Forge: The Judson Press, 1953.

______________, *Ecumenism—Free Church Dilemma.* Valley Forge: The Judson Press, 1968.

Toynbee, Arnold J., *Change and Habit.* New York: Oxford University Press, Inc., 1966.

Tunnard, Christopher and Pushkarev, Boris, *Man-Made America: Chaos or Control?* New Haven: Yale University Press, 1963.

Walker, Daniel D., *Enemy in the Pew.* New York: Harper & Row, Publishers, Inc., 1967.

Ward, Barbara, *The Rich Nations and the Poor Nations.* New York: W. W. Norton & Company, Inc., 1962.

Weatherhead, Leslie D., *When the Lamp Flickers.* Nashville: Abingdon Press, 1948.

Weinberg, Arthur and Lila, eds., *The Muckrakers.* New York: Simon and Schuster, Inc., 1961.

Whitley, Oliver R., *Religious Behavior.* Englewood Cliffs: Prentice-Hall, Inc., 1964.

Whyte, William H., Jr., *The Organization Man.* New York: Simon & Schuster Inc., 1956.

Wickham, E. R., *Encounter with Modern Society*. New York: The Seabury Press, Inc., 1964.

Wilkerson, David and Sherrill, John and Elizabeth, *The Cross and the Switchblade*. New York: Bernard Geis Associates, 1963.

Ungersma, A. J., *The Search for Meaning*. Philadelphia: The Westminster Press, 1961.

Uris, Auren, *The Executive Breakthrough*. New York: Doubleday & Company, Inc., 1967.

Vernon, Raymond, *Metropolis 1985*. Cambridge: Harvard University Press, 1960.

C. General Reference Works:

Book Review Digest
Current Biography
Dissertation Abstracts
Doctoral Dissertations Accepted by American Universities
Encyclopaedia Britannica
Encyclopedia Americana
Guide to Reference Books
International Periodicals Directory
Monthly Catalogue of United States Government Publications
New York Times Index
Publishers' Weekly
Readers' Guide to Periodical Literature
Statesman's Year Book: Statistical and Historical Annual of the States of the World
Vertical File Index
Who's Who in America: A Biographical Dictionary of Notable Living Men and Women of the United States
World Almanac

Appendix 2
Books on Biblical Interpretation

Ackroyd, P. R., and others, eds., *The Cambridge Bible Commentary on the New English Bible.* New York: Cambridge University Press, 1965.

Albright, William F., *Recent Discoveries in Bible Lands.* New York: Funk & Wagnalls, 1936.

Alexander, George M., *The Handbook of Biblical Personalities.* New York: The Seabury Press, Inc., 1962.

Allen, Charles L., *When the Heart Is Hungry.* Westwood: Fleming H. Revell Co., 1955.

Altizer, Thomas J. and Hamilton, William, *Radical Theology and the Death of God.* Indianapolis: The Bobbs-Merrill Company, Inc., 1966.

Bailey, Albert Edward, *Daily Life in Bible Times.* New York: Charles Scribner's Sons, 1943.

Baird, William, *The Corinthian Church – A Biblical Approach to Urban Culture.* Nashville: Abingdon Press, 1964.

Baxter, Edna M., *The Beginnings of Our Religion.* Valley Forge: The Judson Press, 1968.

Bentzen, Aage, *Introduction to the Old Testament,* 2nd. ed. Stockholm: G. E. C. Gads Forlag, 1952.

Berkeley, James P., *Paul and Philippians.* Valley Forge: The Judson Press, 1969.

Bewer, Julius A., *Annotated Bible Series.* New York: Harper & Row, Publishers, Inc., 1949.

Blackwood, Andrew W., *Preaching from the Bible.* Nashville: Abingdon Press, 1941.

Bowman, John Wick, *Prophetic Realism and the Gospel.* Philadelphia: The Westminster Press, 1945.

Briggs, Charles A., *General Introduction to the Study of Holy Scripture.* New York: Charles Scribner's Sons, 1899.

Brown, Francis, and others, *A Hebrew and English Lexicon of the Old Testament.* Oxford: The Clarendon Press, 1952.

Buttrick, George Arthur, ed., *The Interpreter's Bible,* 12 vols. Nashville: Abingdon Press, 1953-1957.

Cadbury, Henry J., *The Book of Acts in History.* New York: Harper & Row, Publishers, Inc., 1955.

Corswant, W., *A Dictionary of Life in Bible Times.* New York: Oxford University Press, 1960.

Cullmann, Oscar, *The Christology of the New Testament.* Philadelphia: The Westminster Press, 1959.

Dentan, Robert C., *The Design of the Scriptures.* New York: McGraw-Hill Book Company, 1960.

Douglas, James D., ed., *The New Bible Dictionary.* Grand Rapids: Wm. B. Eerdmans Publishing Co., 1962.

Driver, S. R., *The Book of Genesis.* Methuen and Company, Ltd., 1911.

Eiselen, Frederick Carl and others, *The Abingdon Bible Commentary.* Nashville: Abingdon Press, 1929.

Ellison, John W., *Nelson's Complete Concordance of the Revised Standard Version Bible.* Camden: Thomas Nelson & Sons, 1957.

Farrar, F. W., *The Bible – Its Meaning and Supremacy.* Longmans, Green, and Company, 1897.

Finegan, Jack, *Bible Antiquities.* 2nd. ed. Princeton: Princeton University Press, 1959.

————————, *Light from the Ancient Past.* Princeton: Princeton University Press, 1946.

Fosdick, Harry E., *The Modern Use of the Bible.* New York: The Macmillan Company, 1925.

Freehof, Solomon B., *Preface to Scripture.* New York: Union of American Hebrew Congregations, 1957.

Gilmour, G. P., *The Memoirs Called Gospels.* Valley Forge: The Judson Press, 1959.

Gladden, Washington, *Who Wrote the Bible?* Boston: Houghton Mifflin Company, 1891.

Glen, J. Stanley, *The Parables of Conflict in Luke.* Philadelphia: The Westminster Press, 1962.

Gordon, Cyrus H., *Introduction to Old Testament Times.* Ventnor Publishing, Inc., 1953.

————————, *The World of the Old Testament.* New York: Doubleday & Company, Inc., 1958.

Grant, Frederick C., *The Gospels: Their Origin and Their Growth.* New York: Harper & Row, Publishers, Inc., 1957.

Grant, Robert M., and Freedman, D. N., *The Secret Sayings of Jesus.* New York: Doubleday & Company, Inc., 1960.

Greenslade, S. L., ed., *The Cambridge History of the Bible.* New York: Cambridge University Press, 1963.

Griffeth, Ross, *Bible and Rural Life.* Cincinnati: Standard Publishing Co., 1937.

Hastings, James, ed., *Dictionary of the Bible.* New York: Charles Scribner's Sons, 1963.

————————, *The Greater Men and Women of the Bible.* Edinburgh: T. & T. Clark, 1913.

Heim, Ralph Daniel, *A Harmony of the Gospels.* Philadelphia: Fortress Press, 1946.

Higginbottom, Sam, *Gospel and the Plow.* New York: The Macmillan Company, 1932.

Hunter, Archibald M., *Introducing the New Testament.* Philadelphia: The Westminster Press, 1957.

Jeremias, Joachim, *The Parables of Jesus.* New York: Charles Scribner's Sons, 1956.

Jordan, Clarence, *The Cotton Patch Version of Paul's Epistles.* New York: Association Press, 1968.

Keck, Leander E., *Mandate to Witness.* Valley Forge: The Judson Press, 1964.

Kee, Howard Clark, *Understanding the New Testament.* Englewood Cliffs: Prentice-Hall, Inc., 1957.

Kirkpatrick, A. F., ed., *Psalms.* New York: Cambridge University Press, 1957.

Klemme, Huber F., *The Bible and Our Common Life.* Philadelphia: (imprint United Church Press) Christian Education Press, 1953.

Knight, George A., *A Christian Theology of the Old Testament.* Richmond: John Knox Press, 1959.

Leavenworth, Lynn, ed., *Great Themes in Theology.* Valley Forge: The Judson Press, 1958.

Linnemann, Eta, *Jesus of the Parables.* New York: Harper & Row, Publishers, Inc., 1966.

Luccock, Halford E., *Communicating the Gospel.* New York: Harper & Row, Publishers, Inc., 1954.

MacKay, Alastair I., *Farming and Gardening in the Bible.* Emmaus, Pa.: Rodale Press, 1951.

Maston, T. B., *The Bible and Race.* Nashville: Broadman Press, 1959.

Maus, Cynthia Pearl, *The Old Testament and the Fine Arts.* New York: Harper & Row, Publishers, Inc., 1954.

May, Herbert G. and Metzger, Bruce M., eds., *The Oxford Annotated Bible with the Apocrypha.* Rev. ed. New York: Oxford University Press, 1965.

Metzger, Bruce M., *The Oxford Concise Concordance to the Revised Standard Version of the Holy Bible.* New York: Oxford University Press, 1962.

________________, *The Text of the New Testament.* New York: Oxford University Press, 1964.

Millard, William B., *The Supplementary Bible.* New York: Vantage Press, 1958.

Miller, Madeleine S. and Miller, J. Lane, *Harper's Bible Dictionary.* New York: Harper & Row, Publishers, Inc., 1952.

Moffat, James, *The Bible.* New York: Harper & Row, Publishers, Inc., 1935.

Mould, Elmer W. K., *Essentials of Bible History.* New York: The Ronald Press Company, 1939.

Neil, William, *Harper's Bible Commentary.* New York: Harper & Row, Publishers, Inc., 1963.

________________, *Modern Man Looks at the Bible.* New York: Association Press, 1958.

Neill, Stephen, *The Interpretation of the New Testament.* New York: Oxford University Press, 1964.

Newman, Jr., Barclay M., *Rediscovering the Book of Revelation.* Valley Forge: The Judson Press, 1968.

Oates, Wayne E., *The Bible in Pastoral Care.* Philadelphia: The Westminster Press, 1953.

Pfeiffer, Robert H., *Introduction to the Old Testament.* New York: Harper & Row, Publishers, Inc., 1948.

Ramm, Bernard, *The Christian View of Science and Scripture.* Grand Rapids: Wm. B. Eerdmans Publishing Co., 1954.

Richardson, Alan, *An Introduction to the Theology of the New Testament.* New York: Harper & Row, Publishers, Inc., 1959.

———, ed., *A Theological Word Book of the Bible.* New York: The Macmillan Company, 1962.

Richardson, Herbert W., *Toward an American Theology.* New York: Harper & Row, Publishers, Inc., 1967.

Robinson, Willard H., *The Parables of Jesus in Their Relation to His Ministry.* Chicago: University of Chicago Press, 1928.

Rowley, H. H., *The Old Testament and Modern Study.* Oxford: The Clarendon Press, 1951.

———, *The Servant of the Lord and Other Essays on the Old Testament.* London: Lutterworth Press, 1952.

Rutenber, Culbert G., *The Reconciling Gospel.* Valley Forge: The Judson Press, 1960.

Sampey, John R., *The Heart of the Old Testament.* Nashville: Broadman Press, 1922.

Sandmel, Samuel, *A Jewish Understanding of the New Testament.* New York: Hebrew-Union College Press, 1957.

Stimpson, George, *A Book About the Bible.* New York: Harper & Row, Publishers, Inc., 1945.

Straton, Hillyer Hawthorne, *A Guide to the Parables of Jesus.* Grand Rapids: Wm. B. Eerdmans Publishing Co., 1959.

Stringfellow, Ervin Edward, *The Gospels.* New York: John S. Swift Company, 1943.

Thielicke, Helmut, *The Ethics of Sex.* New York: Harper & Row, Publishers, Inc., 1964.

———, *How the World Began.* Philadelphia: Fortress Press, 1961.

Tilson, Everett, *Segregation and the Bible.* Nashville: Abingdon Press, 1958.

Wand, J. W. C., *The Authority of the Scriptures.* London: A. R. Mowbray and Company, Ltd., 1949.

Wedel, Theodore O., *The Gospel in a Strange New World.* Philadelphia: The Westminster Press, 1963.

Wright, George E., *Biblical Archaeology,* New and rev. ed. Philadelphia: The Westminster Press, 1963.

Young, Robert, *Analytical Concordance to the Bible.* New York: Funk & Wagnalls, 1936.

Younger, George D., *The Bible Calls for Action.* Philadelphia: The Judson Press, 1959.

Appendix 3
Pope Paul's Address at the United Nations

As we begin Our address to this audience, unique in the world, We wish first to express Our profound gratitude to Mr. Thant, your Secretary-General, for the invitation which he extended to Us to visit the United Nations on the occasion of the twentieth anniversary of this world institution for peace and co-operation among the peoples of all the earth.

Thanks also to the President of the General Assembly, Mr. Amintore Fanfani, who has had such kind words for Us from the very day he took office.

Thanks to all of you here present for your warm welcome. To each one of you We extend Our cordial and deferential greeting. Your friendship has invited Us and admits Us to this meeting; it is as a friend that We appear before you.

In addition to Our personal homage, We bring you that of the Second Vatican Ecumenical Council, now meeting in Rome and represented here by the eminent Cardinals who are accompanying Us.

In their name, as in Our own, to all of you, honour and greeting.

You are all well aware that this meeting between us is of a twofold nature: it bears the stamp both of simplicity and of grandeur. Simplicity, because he who speaks to you is a man like you; he is your brother, and even one of the least among you, representing as you do sovereign States, for he is vested — if it please you so to think of Us — with only a minute and quasi-symbolic temporal sovereignty, only so much as is needed to leave him free to exercise his spiritual mission and to assure all those who treat with him that he is independent of every worldly sovereignty. He has no temporal power, no ambition to compete with you. In point of fact, We have nothing to ask for, no question to raise; at most a wish to express and a permission to request: to serve you, within Our competence, disinterestedly, humbly and in love.

This is the first statement We have to make. As you see, it is so simple that it may seem insignificant to this Assembly, accustomed as it is to dealing with extremely important and difficult matters.

And yet We said to you — and you all feel it — that this moment bears the stamp of a special grandeur. Grandeur for Us, grandeur for you.

First, for Us. Oh! You well know who We are. Whatever your opinion of the Roman Pontiff, you know Our mission: We are the bearer of a message for all mankind. This We are not only in Our own name and in the name of the great Catholic family, but also in the name of those Christian brethren who share the feelings We express here, and particularly of those who charged Us explicitly to be their spokesman here. And like the messenger who, at the end of a long journey, delivers the letter entrusted to him, We are conscious of living a privileged moment — short as it may be — which fulfils a wish We have been carrying in Our heart for nearly twenty centuries. Yes, you do remember. We have been on the way for a long time and We bear with Us a long history; here We celebrate the end of a laborious pilgrimage in search of a colloquy with the whole world, a pilgrimage which began when We were given the command: "Go and bring the good news to all nations." And it is you who represent all nations. Allow Us to tell you that We have a message for you all. Yes! A happy message to deliver to each of you.

(1) We wish Our message first of all to be a moral and solemn ratification of this high Institution. The message comes to Our experience of history. It is as an "expert in humanity" that We bring to this Organization the voices of Our latest Predecessors, those of the whole Catholic Episcopate, and Our own, convinced as We are that this Organization represents the obligatory road of modern civilization and of world peace.

In saying this, We are aware that We are making Our own the voices both of the dead and of the living: of the dead who fell in the terrible wars of the past while dreaming of harmony and world peace; of the living who survived war and already in their hearts condemn those who would try to bring it again; and of still others of the living, the young generations of today going forward confidently in rightful expectation of a better humanity. We also make Our own the voice of the poor, the disinherited, the unfortunate; of those who yearn for justice, for the dignity of life, for freedom, for well-being and for progress. The peoples turn to the United Nations as to the ultimate hope for harmony and peace. We venture to bring here their tribute of honour and hope, together with Our own. And that is why this moment is great for you too.

(2) We know that you are fully aware of this. Listen now to the rest of Our message. It looks wholly to the future. The building you have made must never again fall in ruins; it must be perfected and conformed to the demands world history will make. You mark a stage in the development of mankind: henceforth no turning back, you must go forward.

To the majority of States, no longer able to ignore each other, you offer an extremely simple and fruitful form of coexistence. It is this: first of all you recognize and distinguish *one another*. You do not, of course, confer existence upon States, but you qualify each nation as worthy to sit in the ordered assembly of the peoples: you grant to each national sovereign community a recognition of high moral and juridical value, and you guarantee it an honourable international citizenship. This in itself is a great service to the cause of mankind: clearly to define and to honour the national entities of the world community, and to establish them in a juridical status which entitles them to be recognized and respected by all and from which there may derive an ordered and stable system of international life. You give sanction to the great principle that relations between the peoples should be regulated by reason, by justice, by law, by negotiation; not by force nor by violence nor by war, neither by fear nor by fraud.

So it should be. And allow Us to congratulate you on having had the wisdom to leave the door to this Assembly open to the young peoples, to the States which have but lately attained national independence and freedom; their presence here is proof of the universality and magnanimity which inform the principles of this Institution.

So it should be. This is what We praise and what We wish for you, and, as you see, these virtues We ascribe to you do not come from without. We draw them from within, from the very genius of your Institution.

(3) Your Charter goes even further; and Our message goes forward with it. You exist and work to unite the nations, to associate the States together. Let Us use the formula: to bring togther *one and another.* You are an Association. You are a bridge between the peoples. You are a network of relations among the States. We are tempted to say that your character in some sort reflects in the temporal order what our Catholic Church seeks to be in the spiritual order — unique and universal. Nothing higher can be imagined on the natural level, in the ideological structure of mankind. Your vocation is to bring not only some of the peoples, but all of the peoples, to fraternize. A difficult undertaking? No doubt. But such is the undertaking, your most noble undertaking. Who does not see the need thus progressively to set up a world authority, able to act effectively on the juridical and political plane?

Once more We repeat Our wish for you: go forward. We shall say more: strive to bring back among you any who may have left you; consider means of calling into your pact of brotherhood, in honour and loyalty, those who do not yet share in it. Act so that those still outside will desire and deserve the confidence of all; and then be generous in granting it. And you, who have the good fortune and the honour to sit in this Assembly of the peaceful community, hear Us; so act that there may never be an attempt on the mutual confidence which unites you and enables you to do good and great things, that it may never be betrayed.

(4) The reason for this wish, which might be said to pertain to the structure of your Organization, leads Us to complete it with other formulas. They are these: let no one, as a member of your Association, be superior to the others: *not one above another.* This is the formula of equality. We well know that there are other factors to be considered besides that of mere membership of this body. But equality, too, is a part of its constitution; not that you are equal, but that here you make yourselves equal. And it may be that for several among you this is an act of high virtue; allow Us to say this to you, We who represent a religion which works salvation through the humility of its divine Founder. It is impossible to be a brother if one is not humble. For it is pride, however inevitable it may seem, which provokes tensions, struggles for prestige, predominance, colonialism, selfishness; it is pride that shatters brotherhood.

(5) And here Our message reaches its highest point. Negatively, at first. It is the word you are expecting from Us and We cannot utter it without being conscious of its gravity and solemnity: *never again one against another,* never, never again! Is it not to this end above all that the United Nations was born: against war and for peace? Listen to the lucid words of a great man now departed, John Kennedy, who declared four years ago: "Mankind must put an end to war, or war will put an end to mankind." There is no need of long speeches to proclaim the supreme finality of this Institution. Suffice it to recall that the blood of millions of men, that countless and unheard-of sufferings, that useless massacres and fearful

ruins have sealed the pact uniting you, with a vow which must change the future history of the world: never again war, war never again! Peace, it is peace, which must guide the destiny of the peoples and of all mankind!

Thanks to you, glory to you, who for twenty years have laboured for peace and have even given illustrious victims to this holy cause. Thanks to you and glory to you for the conflicts you have prevented and for those you have settled. The results of your efforts for peace, up to these last days, even if not yet decisive, deserve that We venture to interpret the feelings of the whole world and in its name express to you both congratulations and gratitude.

You, gentlemen, have done and are doing a great work: you are teaching men peace. The United Nations is the great school where that education is acquired, and We are here in the *Aula Magna* of that school. Whoever takes a place here becomes both pupil and teacher in the art of building peace. And when you leave this hall, the world looks to you as to the architects, the builders of peace.

Peace, as you know, is built not only by means of politics and the balance of forces and interests. It is built with the spirit, with ideas, with works of peace. You are labouring at this great work. But you are as yet only at the beginning of your labours. Will the world ever succeed in changing the exclusive and bellicose state of mind which up to now has woven so much of its history? This is hard to foresee; but it is easy to affirm that we must resolutely take the road towards a new history, a peaceful history, one that will be truly and fully human, the very history God promised to men of goodwill. The roads to it are mapped for you: the first is that of disarmament.

If you wish to be brothers, let the weapons fall from your hands. You cannot love with offensive weapons in your hands. Even before they cause victims and ruins, weapons, especially the terrible weapons modern science has given you, beget bad dreams, nourish bad feelings, create nightmares, mistrust and sombre resolves; they exact enormous expenditures; they bring to a halt projects of useful work undertaken in solidarity; they warp the psychology of peoples. So long as man remains the weak, changeable and even wicked being that he often shows himself to be, defensive arms will, alas! be necessary. But you, your courage and valour spur you to study ways of guaranteeing the security of international life without recourse to arms: this is an aim worthy of your efforts, this is what the peoples expect of you. This is what must be attained. And for this, unanimous trust in this Institution must grow; its authority must grow; and the goal, it is to be hoped, will then be reached. Then you will win the gratitude of all peoples, relieved of the crushing expense of armaments and delivered from the nightmare of ever-imminent war.

We know — and how could We not rejoice in the knowledge? — that many among you looked with favour upon the invitation in the cause of peace that We addressed to all States from Bombay last December: to devote to the benefit of the developing countries at least part of the savings which can be realized by reducing armaments. We here renew that invitation, with the confidence your sentiments of humanity and generosity inspire in Us.

(6) To speak of humanity and generosity is to echo another constituent principle of the United Nations, the very highest: you are labouring here not only to exorcise conflicts between States; but to make States capable of working *one for another*. You are not satisfied with making coexistence

between nations easier; you are taking a much greater step forward, a step deserving of Our praise and Our support: you are organizing brotherly co-operation among the peoples. Here a system of solidarity is being set up, so that the high aims of civilized order may win the unanimous and ordered support of the whole family of peoples, to the good of all and everyone. This is what is most beautiful in the United Nations; this is its most truly human face; this is the ideal which mankind dreams of on its pilgrimage through time; this is the world's greatest hope. We presume to say that this is the reflection of God's design – a transcendent design and full of love – for the progress of the human society on earth, a reflection in which We see the message of the Gospel, which is heavenly, become earthly. Indeed, it seems to Us that here We catch an echo of the voice of Our Predecessors, particularly of Pope John XXIII, whose message of *Pacem in Terris* evoked among you so honourable and significant a response.

What you proclaim here are the fundamental rights and duties of man, his dignity, his freedom, and above all his religious freedom. We feel that you are the interpreters of what is highest in human wisdom, We would almost say, of its sacred character. For it is above all the life of man that is in question and the life of man is sacred; no one may dare offend it. It is in your Assembly that respect for life, even in so far as the great problem of the birth rate is concerned, must find its highest affirmation and its most reasoned defence. Your task is to ensure that there is enough bread on the table of mankind, and not to favour an artificial control of births, which would be irrational, in order to lessen the number of guests at the banquet of life.

But it is not enough to feed the starving; each man must also be assured of a life consistent with his dignity. And this is what you are striving to achieve. Is this not the realization, before our eyes and thanks to you, of the prophetic utterance so well suited to your Institution: "They shall beat their swords into ploughshares and their spears into pruning-hooks" (Isaiah 2:4)? Are you not using the prodigious energies of the earth and the magnificent inventions of science, no longer as instruments of death, but as tools of life for the new era of mankind?

We know with what growing intensity and effectiveness the United Nations and its related world agencies render help to Governments which need it to speed their economic and social progress.

We know how ardently you work to conquer illiteracy and to spread culture throughout the world; to give men proper and modern medical assistance; to put at man's service the marvellous resources of science and of the techniques of organization. All this is magnificent and deserving of everyone's praise and support, including Our own.

We Ourself would also like to set an example, even though the smallness of Our means is inadequate to the practical and quantitative needs. We wish to intensify the efforts of Our charitable institutions against the world's hunger and to meet its chief needs. It is thus, and in no other way, that peace is built.

(7) One word more, gentlemen, one last word: this edifice you are building does not rest upon purely material and earthly foundations, for it would then be a house built on sand; above all, it rests on our consciences. Yes! the moment of "conversion" has come, of personal transformation, of inner renewal. We must accustom ourselves to think of man in a new way; and in a new way also of men's life in common; finally,

in a new way of the paths of history and the destiny of the world; in accordance with the words of Saint Paul, to "put on the new man which, after God, is created in righteousness, and the holiness of truth" (Ephesians 4:24).

Now the hour for a halt is upon us, a moment of meditation, of reflection, almost of prayer; a moment to think anew of our common origin, our history, our common destiny. Never before has there been such a need for an appeal to the moral conscience of man as there is today, in an era marked by such human progress. For the peril comes neither from progress nor from science; on the contrary, properly used, they could resolve many of the grave problems which beset mankind. The real peril is in man, who has at hand ever more powerful instruments, suited as much to destruction as to the highest conquests.

In a word, the edifice of modern civilization must be built on spiritual principles, which alone can not only support it, but also illuminate and animate it. And it is Our conviction, as you know, that these indispensable principles of higher wisdom can rest only on faith in God. The unknown God of whom Saint Paul spoke to the Athenians on the Areopagus? Unknown to those who, without realizing it, yet sought Him and had Him near them, as happens to so many men of our century? . . . To us, in any case, and to all those who receive the ineffable revelation which Christ has given us of Him, He is the living God, the Father of all men.[1]

Notes

CHAPTER 1

[1] Joseph Glanvill, *Seasonable Defence of Preaching* (1678).

[2] Ralph Nichols, "Do We Know How to Listen? Practical Help in a Modern Age," *The Speech Teacher,* March, 1961, pp. 118-124.

[3] *Ibid.*

CHAPTER 2

[1] Booker T. Washington, *Up from Slavery* (New York: The Sun Dial Press, 1937), p. 219.

CHAPTER 3

[1] Lewis Copeland and Lawrence Lamm, eds., *The World's Great Speeches* (2nd ed. rev.; New York: Dover Publications, Inc., 1958), p. 670.

[2] Henry C. Fish, *History and Repository of Pulpit Eloquence* (New York: M. W. Dodd, 1856), Vol. I, p. 193.

[3] Cited in A. Craig Baird, ed., *Representative American Speeches: 1938-1939* (New York: H. W. Wilson Co., 1939), Vol. 13, No. 3, p. 226, with permission to reproduce from Dr. Harry Emerson Fosdick.

[4] Daniel E. Wheeler, ed., *Life and Writings of Thomas Paine* (New York: Vincent Parke and Company, 1908), Vol. I, pp. 101-102.

Albert J. Beveridge, *The Meaning of the Times* (Indianapolis: The Bobbs-Merrill Company, Inc., 1908), p. 43. Reprinted by permission of the publishers, The Bobbs-Merrill Company, Inc.

[6] Roy P. Basler, ed., *The Collected Works of Abraham Lincoln* (New Brunswick, N. J.: Rutgers University Press, 1953), Vol. II, pp. 461-462.

[7] Charles Henry Woolbert, "Principles of Persuasion and Method Analysis," *The Quarterly Journal of Speech Education,* Vol. V (March, 1919), p. 107.

[8] See Otis M. Walter, "Toward an Analysis of Motivation," *The Quarterly Journal of Speech,* Vol. XLI (October, 1955), pp. 271-278.

[9] John Dewey, *How We Think* (New York: D. C. Heath & Company, 1910), p. 9.

[10] *Memorial Addresses in the Congress of the United States and Tributes in Eulogy of John Fitzgerald Kennedy* (Washington: United States Government Printing Office, 1964), pp. 227-228. Hereafter referred to as *Memorial Addresses.*
[11] *Ibid.,* p. 228.
[12] *Ibid.*
[13] *Ibid.*
[14] *Ibid.*
[15] Adlai E. Stevenson, *Putting First Things First: A Democratic View* (New York: Random House, Inc., 1960), pp. 79-80. Reprinted by permission of the publisher.
[16] John Bigelow, ed., *The Life of Benjamin Franklin* (2nd ed. rev.; Philadelphia: J. B. Lippincott and Co., 1879), Vol. III, p. 394.
[17] *Never Again War!* (New York: United Nations Office of Public Information, 1965), p. 33.
[18] *Ibid.,* pp. 33-34.
[19] *Memorial Addresses,* p. 227.
[20] See *Congressional Record, House* (April 19, 1951), pp. 4123-4125.
[21] *Ibid.*
[22] Richard K. Cralle, ed., *The Works of John C. Calhoun* (New York: D. Appleton and Comany, 1883), Vol. II, pp. 228-229.
[23] *Never Again War!,* p. 31.

CHAPTER 5

[1] Longinus, *On Great Writing (On the Sublime),* G. M. A. Grube, trans. (Indianapolis: The Liberal Arts Press, Inc., © 1957). Reprinted by permission of the Liberal Arts Press Division of The Bobbs-Merrill Company, Inc.
[2] Charles Henry Woolbert, "Speaking and Writing — A Study of Differences," *The Quarterly Journal of Speech Education,* Vol. VIII (June, 1922), pp. 271-285.
[3] Hugh Blair, *Lectures on Rhetoric and Belles Lettres* (Philadelphia: T. Ellwood Zell, 1833), pp. 101-102.
[4] Arthur Schopenhauer, *A Series of Essays,* T. Bailey Saunders, trans. (New York: A. L. Burt Publishers, n.d.), pp. 298, 301.
[5] Austin Phelps, *English Style in Public Discourse* (New York: Charles Scribner's Sons, 1888), p. 5.
[6] Quintilian, *The Institutio Oratoria,* H. E. Butler, trans. (New York: G. P. Putnam's Sons, 1921), Vol. VIII, Preface 32.
[7] Schopenhauer, *op. cit.,* p. 31.
[8] William Shedd, ed., *The Complete Works of Samuel Taylor Coleridge* (New York: Harper & Row, Publishers, Inc., 1853), Vol. IV, p. 343.
[9] Thomas B. Reed, ed., *Modern Eloquence* (Philadelphia: John D. Morris and Company, 1900), Vol. IV, p. 225.
[10] Frederic May Holland, *Frederick Douglass* (New York: Funk & Wagnalls, 1891), p. 210.
[11] Reed, *op. cit.,* p. 258.
[12] Clarence Edward Macartney, ed., *Great Sermons of the World* (Boston: The Stratford Company, Publishers, 1926), pp. 246-247.
[13] Henry C. Fish, *History and Repository of Pulpit Eloquence* (New York: M. W. Dodd, 1857), Vol. II, pp. 458-459.
[14] Macartney, *op. cit.,* p. 115.
[15] *Ibid.,* p. 493.

[16] Joseph Mazzini, *Life and Writings of Joseph Mazzini* (London: Smith, Elder, and Company, 1891), Vol. V, p. 165.

[17] *Memorial Addresses,* p. 321.

[18] *Ibid.,* p. 375.

[19] Chauncey A. Goodrich, ed., *Select British Eloquence* (Indianapolis: The Bobbs-Merrill Company, Inc., © 1963), p. 267. Reprinted by permission of the publishers.

[20] *Ibid.,* p. 107.

[21] *Memorial Addresses,* p. 209.

[22] *Ibid.,* p. 228.

[23] *Ibid.*

[24] Lord Macaulay, *Critical and Historical Essays* (Boston: Houghton Mifflin Company, 1900), Vol. I, pp. 644-645.

[25] *Ibid.,* p. 645.

[26] Daniel Webster, *The Works of Daniel Webster,* 13th ed. (Boston: Little, Brown and Company, 1864), Vol. I, p. 133.

[27] *Memorial Addresses,* p. 211.

[28] Macartney, *op. cit.,* p. 39.

[29] G. Paul Butler, ed., *Best Sermons, 1951-1952* (New York: The Macmillan Company, 1952), p. 64.

[30] *Orations of American Orators* (rev. ed.; New York: The Colonial Press, 1900), Vol. I, p. 13.

[31] Fish, *op. cit.,* Vol. II, p. 78.

[32] *Memorial Addresses,* p. 1.

[33] Macartney, *op. cit.,* p. 90.

[34] J. B. McClure, ed., *Mistakes of Ingersoll* (Chicago: Rhodes & McClure Publishing Company, 1898), p. 242.

[35] *Memorial Addresses,* p. 402.

[36] Butler, *op. cit.,* p. 56.

[37] *Memorial Addresses,* p. 143.

[38] *Orations of American Orators,* Vol. I, pp. 58-59.

[39] Butler, *op. cit.,* p. 162.

[40] *Ibid.,* p. 170.

[41] Goodrich, *op. cit.,* p. 363.

[42] *Memorial Addresses,* p. 188.

[43] Goodrich, *op. cit.,* p. 388.

[44] *Memorial Addresses,* p. 142.

[45] Butler, *op. cit.,* p. 299.

[46] Goodrich, *op. cit.,* p. 135.

[47] *Never Again War!,* p. 37.

[48] *Memorial Addresses,* p. 228.

[49] *Ibid.,* p. 365.

[50] A. Craig Baird, ed., *Representative American Speeches: 1957-1958* (New York: H. W. Wilson Co., 1958), Vol. 30, p. 177.

[51] *Memorial Addresses,* p. 225.

[52] Roy P. Basler, ed., *The Collected Works of Abraham Lincoln,* Vol. III, p. 279.

[53] Reed, *op. cit.,* Vol. I, pp. 210-211.

[54] Daniel Mallory, ed., *The Life and Speeches of the Hon. Henry Clay* (New York: A. S. Barnes & Burr, 1853), p. 535.

[55] *Memorial Addresses,* p. 197.

[56] Fish, *op. cit.,* Vol. I, p. 351.

[57] Macartney, *op. cit.,* p. 459.

[58] Goodrich, *op. cit.*, p. 936.
[59] *Memorial Addresses,* pp. 572-573.
[60] *Ibid.*, p. 242.
[61] Fish, *op. cit.*, Vol. II, p. 387.
[62] Macartney, *op. cit.*, p. 500.
[63] *Memorial Addresses,* p. 573.
[64] *Ibid.*, p. 574.
[65] *Ibid.*, p. 182.
[66] *Ibid.*, p. 309.
[67] Elizabeth Cady Stanton and others, eds., *History of Woman Suffrage,* 2nd ed. (New York: Charles Mann, 1889), p. 71.
[68] Macartney, *op. cit.*, p. 203.
[69] Fish, *op. cit.*, Vol. I, p. 158.
[70] See Reed, *op. cit.*, Vol. I, p. 113.
[71] Basler, *op. cit.*, Vol. VII, p. 23.
[72] *Memorial Addresses,* p. 227.
[73] Ralph Waldo Emerson, *Nature, Addresses and Lectures* (Boston: Houghton Mifflin Company, 1884), p. 110.
[74] *Memorial Addresses,* p. 75.
[75] *Ibid.*, p. 518.
[76] Reed, *op. cit.*, Vol. III, p. 907.
[77] *Ibid.*, Vol. I, p. 68.
[78] *Ibid.*, Vol. VI, p. 948.
[79] *Ibid.*, Vol. VIII, p. 637.
[80] Lewis Copeland and Lawrence Lamm, eds., *The World's Great Speeches* (New York: Dover Publications, Inc., 1958), p. 732.
[81] *Memorial Addresses,* p. 235.
[82] *Ibid.*, p. 2.
[83] *Ibid.*, p. 180.
[84] Fish, *op. cit.*, Vol. II, p. 517.
[85] Butler, *op. cit.*, p. 228.
[86] Goodrich, *op. cit.*, p. 293.
[87] *Memorial Addresses,* p. 6.
[88] *Orations of American Orators,* Vol. I, p. 23.
[89] Booker T. Washington, *Up from Slavery,* pp. 221-222.
[90] Baird, *op. cit., 1938-1939,* p. 231. Used by permission of Dr. Harry Emerson Fosdick.
[91] *Congressional Record, House,* Vol. 97, Part 3 (April 19, 1951), p. 4125.
[92] Macartney, *op. cit.*, p. 487.
[93] Basler, *op. cit.*, Vol. II, p. 461.
[94] Butler, *op. cit.*, p. 208.

CHAPTER 6

[1] Cicero, *Brutus,* xxxvii., cited *The Loeb Classical Library,* G. L. Hendrickson, trans. (Cambridge: Harvard University Press, 1939), p. 125.
[2] *Ibid.*, lix, p. 185.
[3] *Ibid.*, lx, p. 185.
[4] Chauncey A. Goodrich, ed., *Select British Eloquence,* p. 577.
[5] *Ibid.*, p. 237.
[6] *Ibid.*, p. 636.
[7] *Ibid.*, p. 460.
[8] Booker T. Washington, *Up from Slavery,* p. 243.
[9] *Ibid.*, pp. 242-243.

[10] Thomas Sheridan, *A Course of Elocution* (New York: Benjamin Blom, Inc., 1968), p. 5.

[11] *Hamlet,* III, ii.

[12] *Ibid.*

[13] Washington, *op. cit.*, pp. 243-244.

APPENDIX 3

[1] *Never Again War!* (New York: Office of Public Information, United Nations, © 1965), pp. 31-43.